GROWING IN THE WORD

GROWING IN THE WORD

How to become the Christian God wants you to be

Hilary Latham

Terra Nova Publications Ltd
Bristol

First published 1999

The publishers acknowledge with appreciation financial assistance
toward the publication of this book, granted by The Drummond Trust,
3 Pitt Terrace, Stirling.

British Library Cataloguing in Publication Data.
A catalogue record for this book is available from the British Library.

ISBN   1 901949 02 8

Printed and bound in Great Britain by The Cromwell Press
Aintree Avenue, Trowbridge, Wiltshire.
Published in Great Britain by Terra Nova Publications Ltd
P.O. Box 2400, Bradford on Avon, Wiltshire BA15 2YN
Registered Office: 21 St.Thomas Street, Bristol BS1 6JS

Contents

Introduction

This book is intended to meet two needs. Those using the study course *Towards Christian Maturity* will find that it usefully supplements the material contained in the course manual. *Growing in the Word* is also designed to be of use to all Christians who have made a personal commitment to the Lord Jesus Christ, have begun to know something of the Holy Spirit's power, and who want to grow in mature and confident faith in the promises of God. Whether we have just completed an introductory course on Christianity or have been Christians much longer, we all need to know and understand His covenant with His people. We need to learn what He requires of us; how to discern His voice, and how to walk in obedience to Him and so enjoy His blessing in every area of life. God wants us to have life abundantly! Understanding the key biblical themes in this book will begin to equip the believer with that armoury of knowledge of the word which is so necessary for growth in discipleship. The author does not attempt to answer every question about each theme, but rather to provide a sound, concise introduction to each element of biblical teaching covered.

Chapter One

THE INTEGRITY OF THE WORD

"It is written, 'Man shall not live by bread alone, but by every [rhema] *word that proceeds from the mouth of God.'"* Matthew 4:4

In the magazine *Prophecy Today*, Clifford Hill has written, 'The real battle today is for the Bible as the word of God. It is only those who are prepared to stand firm upon His word who will be able to survive the coming storms as the shaking of the nations intensifies.'[1] The Bible is the foundation of our faith. It does not simply *contain* the word of God: it *is* the word of God. It is the manual for life, the manufacturer's handbook and, as such, it is essential that we should know it well if we are to live life successfully.

1 Samuel 3:1 says, '...the word of the Lord was rare in those days; there was no widespread revelation.' What a sad state of affairs! No wonder Israel was in a mess—they were defeated by the Philistines, and the ark of God had been stolen from them. However, God was merciful and gave them a godly prophet, Samuel, to speak His word to the people.

Amos 8:11 speaks of a coming famine of the word. Perhaps we are in danger of allowing other things to take the place of the word of God in our lives. Sometimes we seek after experiences as a substitute for the word. Then we may be in danger of becoming 'children, tossed to and fro and carried about with every wind of doctrine' (Ephesians 4:14). Experience is fine, as long as it accords with the word of God.

Another danger warned of is the replacing of the central place of the word by tradition. In Mark 7:13, Jesus speaks of, 'making the word of God of no effect through your tradition.' Religious traditions often bring people into a sense of condemnation and bondage. An example of this is what is sometimes termed 'worm theology'.

9

This says, 'I am worth nothing. I am just a sinner who is not worthy to stand before the Lord.' This was true before we become Christians, but is contrary to what the word says about us *after* we receive Jesus. The word tells us that then, by faith in Jesus, we are cleansed of all our sin and made righteous. Colossians 2:20–23 describes some of the regulations which 'self-imposed religion' has added to the gospel and which Paul says are of no value in checking the indulgences of the flesh. Unscriptural traditions include a mistaken equating of poverty with holiness, and denial that healings and miracles occur today. Beware of 'religious' traditions that are not supported by the Bible!

A testament is a document by which a person declares his will, and God has declared His will in *both* the Old Testament and the New Testament. The word of God is the will of God. Anything that is contrary to His word cannot be His will. We must become word based people in order to live according to the will of God. The Bible teaches us about God's nature and His dealings with men. In 2 Timothy 3:16 we learn that, 'All Scripture is given by inspiration of God, and is profitable for doctrine, for reproof, for correction, for instruction in righteousness.' The Greek word for inspiration of God is *theopneustos* which means 'God-breathed'. Until God breathed into Adam he had no life. When we get the word in us we are getting God's life in us. Jesus said, 'The words [*rhemata*] that I speak to you are spirit, and they are life' (John 6:63b).

The English 'word' translates two biblical Greek words of different significance— *logos* and *rhema*. *Logos* is used to describe an expression of thought, saying or statement, the revealed will of God. It is the written word of God; the general word of God; God's principles; moral precepts, declarations, doctrine and teaching. It is also the title of the Son of God. In John 1:1 we read, 'In the beginning was the Word (*logos*), and the Word was with God and the Word was God.' John 1:14 says, 'and the Word became flesh and dwelt among us.' Hebrews 1:1–2 says, 'God, who at various times and in various ways spoke in time past to the fathers by the prophets, has in these last days spoken to us by His Son....' Jesus and his word are one. When we read the Bible, it is Jesus speaking to us. In John 14:10b he says, 'The words that I speak to you I do not speak on My own authority; but the Father who dwells in Me does the works.'

'Rhema' is used to describe a word which is spoken. It is the word of God which has become a living reality to you. It is the specific word of God to you, when the **word** becomes **a word to you**. It is not possible to stand in faith on the *logos*, but only on the *rhema* word which has entered your heart and has become reality. In Matthew 4:4 Jesus said, "It is written, 'Man shall not live by bread alone, but by every [*rhema*] word that proceeds from the mouth of God.'" To live by the word is a way of life. It is by meditating the word that it becomes *rhema* to us. Speaking the *rhema* word of God releases the power of God. Luke 1:37 [AMP]: 'For with God nothing is ever impossible, and no word from God shall be without power or impossible of fulfilment.'

The word of God stands supreme. It is our final authority. If circumstances or desires conflict with the word of God, it is the word that must be believed and obeyed. 'For You have magnified Your word above all Your name' (Psalm 138:2b); or, 'You have exalted above all else Your name and Your word, and You have magnified Your word above all Your name' [AMP]. Your word is who you are; it represents your integrity. This is why the City of London Stock Exchange had as its motto 'My word is my bond.' Your name is your reputation. R.T. Kendall says, 'God is more concerned about His integrity than His reputation.' God's word represents His integrity: He is obligated to His word. There is no higher authority. The word of God never changes. 'The word of our God stands forever' (Isaiah 40:8). It doesn't matter what conventions say; it doesn't matter what current fashions dictate; it doesn't matter what other people are doing: the word of God does not change. 'Forever, O LORD, Your word is settled [*lit.* 'stands firm'] in heaven' (Psalm 119:89). God will not change what He has said. 'My covenant I will not break, Nor alter the word that has gone out of My lips' (Psalm 89:34). His word is completely reliable. 'Heaven and earth will pass away, but My words will by no means pass away' (Matthew 24:35).

The word of God is powerful; it creates and destroys. We shall look at this in greater detail later. The Bible shows us how the

11

world was made by God speaking the word. Jesus is 'upholding all things by the word [*rhema*] of His power' (Hebrews 1:3). Note that it is the *word of his power*— not the power of his word. The word is the vehicle which carries the power of God. Jesus taught his disciples the importance of what they spoke by demonstrating the power carried by the word, when he cursed the fig tree. He healed people and cast out demonic spirits *with a word*. Speaking God's word causes it to become a spiritual power force for life or death. The authority is in the word.

God's word is truth. 'Every word of God is pure' (Proverbs 30:5). 'The entirety of Your word is truth, And every one of Your righteous judgements endures for ever' (Psalm 119:160). 'The entrance of Your word gives light; It gives understanding to the simple' (Psalm 119:130). Revelation comes by studying the word. It is by the word that we renew our minds. Our minds are programmed by the world around us, and need to be renewed in order to enable us to live according to God's standards. In John 17:17 Jesus prayed, 'Sanctify them by Your truth. Your word is truth.' In Ephesians, the process by which Jesus sanctifies us, his church, is likened to washing it: '...that He might sanctify and cleanse her [the Church] with the washing of water by the word' (Ephesians 5:26). In John 15:3, Jesus tells his disciples that they are clean because of the word he has spoken to them. James states that the word, when 'implanted' into us—in other words when it becomes part of us—is able to save our souls (see James 1:21). The soul is the mind, will and emotions. It is the mind and emotions which are so often swayed by circumstances, and destabilised by Satan's lies and deceit. The word can hold us steady in conflict. The word can purify our thinking (see Psalm 119:9). It enables us to test all things and discern good from evil. It must become the plumb line (or spirit-level!) by which we decide what is right.

How often do we think we would be all right if only we had more faith? There is only one way to get faith: that is by hearing the word. Romans 10:17 tells us, 'So then faith comes by hearing, and hearing by the word of God.' The tense used here is the continuous tense. It means hearing, and hearing, and hearing the word of God. There is a difference between hearing and reading. Reading brings revelation, but hearing the word, taught under the anointing, brings faith. In fact, *speaking the word to ourselves* increases our faith. By speaking it, I am talking to my own spirit within me.

Knowing the word is the only way to overcome Satan; it is the key to victorious living. Satan's chief weapons against us are lies and deceit. The word is truth, and Jesus said, 'You shall know the truth, and the truth shall make you free' (John 8:32). By knowing the word we can recognise the voice of Satan trying to bring doubt and fear on us and, aware that he is a liar, we can reject his thoughts. No wonder Satan hates the word and will do everything in his power to steal it from us. In the parable of the sower, Jesus explained, 'The sower sows the word. And these are the ones by the wayside where the word is sown. When they hear, Satan comes immediately and takes away the word that was sown in their hearts.' (Mark 4:14,15). Satan does not want the word to take root in our hearts where it can bring forth fruit. He knows that, as it was with Jesus, it is by the word that we can defeat him. When he was tempted in the wilderness, Jesus dealt with the temptation by stating, 'It is written...' (Matthew 4:4,7,10). Then, it says, the devil left him. We must know the word if we are to overcome temptation. It is 'the sword of the Spirit' (Ephesians 6:17). And Hosea said, 'My people are destroyed for lack of knowledge' (Hosea 4:6). Satan can attack us because of our ignorance of the word. He knows that it is the word that defeats him. He will do everything in his power to stop us from studying it and meditating it.

It has been wisely observed that every battle we face concerns the word, and whether or not we build our lives on the faithfulness and integrity of God.

We are appointed to bear fruit. This is the way we can be fully pleasing to Him. Only mature and healthy trees bear fruit. Jesus says we will do this if we abide in him and his words abide in us (John 15:7,8). The amplified version says, 'If you live in Me—abide vitally united to Me—and My words remain in you and continue to live in your hearts, ask whatever you will and it shall be done for you. When you bear (produce) much fruit, My Father is honored and glorified; and you show and prove yourselves to be true followers of Mine' [AMP].

GROWING IN THE WORD

If we let the word of God become *rhema* in our lives, we can speak the word into every situation in our lives and live in victory. It is what God says directly to us that becomes spirit and life. As we allow the word to go from our minds, where it brings intellectual satisfaction, into our spirits, so it brings life. When things become difficult and we are under pressure, that is when what is in our hearts is revealed. It comes out of our mouth! Let it be the word of God. Matthew 4:4 says: 'Man shall not live by bread alone, but by every word that proceeds from the mouth of God.' And in Proverbs 4:22, 'For they [God's words] are life to those who find them, and health to all their flesh.' When the word of God is born in us we will begin to take back more and more ground that the devil has stolen from us in every area of our lives. The devil can do nothing with the man or woman who knows the word, walks in the word, and is committed to responding to every attack, every obstacle and every problem by using the word. Living according to God's word is the secret of success. (See Psalm 1:2,3.)

[1] Used by permission. September/October 1997 issue; Vol.13, No.5

Chapter Two

THE TRIPARTITE NATURE OF MAN :
BODY, SOUL AND SPIRIT

*I say then: Walk in the Spirit, and you shall not
fulfill the lust of the flesh.*   Galatians 5:16

When God created man, He created him in His own image (see
Genesis 1:27.) Thus, every man or woman is not only a body, but
also has a spirit. Each of us lives in a body, and has a soul — the
soul comprising mind, will and emotions. This scriptural truth was
one of the most important teachings I ever received. So many things
that I had not previously understood made sense, once I understood
the difference between *soul* and *spirit*. It might be asked, for example, how one could be righteous before God, notwithstanding the
fact that one still sins. It is because the part of us which becomes
born again and has eternal life and will one day live in heaven with
God, is the *spirit*. This, by the gift and grace of God, is made righteous. However, we still have our old *souls*, which we have to train
in righteousness, by exercising our wills — making them come into
line with our renewed spirits. This is the process of sanctification.
Understanding this, we can see what Paul meant when, in Philippians
2:12, he says, 'work out your own salvation with fear and trem-
bling.'
    Hebrews 4:12 tells us that the word of God divides between
the soul and the spirit, thus clearly distinguishing between the two.
When man was created, he was made in the image of God. His
spirit, soul and body were perfectly integrated at the time of creation. When God told Adam that, in the day that he ate of the tree of
the knowledge of good and evil, he would surely die, the Hebrew
construction means, 'in dying you shall die', i.e. you will die spir-

itually immediately, and die physically over a period of time. Thus, being descended from Adam, and having his nature, we are born with dead spirits, and with a body which is programmed ultimately to die.

Each part of us relates to a different realm. The body relates to the physical realm, and the voice of the body is feelings. Our five physical senses tell us about the physical world we live in. The soul relates to the intellectual realm; the religious, political and philosophical world. By 'religion' is meant a man-made system of rules and observances, whereas real Christianity is about a relationship with God our Father. The voice of the soul is reason. However, God does not reveal Himself to the intellect but to the spirit. The mind, the will and the emotions together constitute the soul. The mind stands between the body and the spirit. It is here that the battle takes place in the believer. Satan cannot affect our spirits once we are born again, but he will try to subvert our minds with his thoughts. **In order to live as we should as Christians, we have to renew our minds so that they are in agreement with our renewed spirits.** This is why, in his letter to the Romans, Paul laments the fact that he does not do the good that he would do, and the evil that he would not do, he does. His will is still, to some extent, submitted to his 'flesh man'— his mind, his emotions and his body. But he finishes this discussion with the statement, 'There is therefore now no condemnation to those who are in Christ Jesus, who do not walk according to the flesh, but according to the spirit' (Romans 8:1). Our wills determine what we do. We are free to make choices: God will not override our wills. So we have to train our wills to be totally submitted to God.

The spirit is our 'innermost being' which, when made alive in Christ Jesus, is the new man to which Paul refers. This relates to God; it is God-conscious. In 1 Corinthians 2, Paul tells us that the Holy Spirit reveals to our spirits the things of God. The voice of the spirit is conscience. Proverbs 20:27 says, 'The spirit of a man is the lamp of the LORD, searching all the inner depths of his heart.' The heart usually refers to the human spirit or soul, or both together. Although we are born with a dead spirit, this is made alive when we are born again (see Ephesians 2:1). Our spirit, then, is made righteous and we have become a new creation in Christ. (See 2 Corinthians 5:17).

Peter Michell, in his book *Inherent Power*, makes this clear with the helpful diagrams reproduced here[1]:

Before being born-again:
spirit in death and darkness

After new birth:
spirit alive and indwelt
by the Holy Spirit

When we are born again, the Holy Spirit comes and lives in our human spirit. However it is possible to be born again and not realise the source of power within. "If we live according to the understanding of only our minds or if we live in response only to the strong desires of our bodies, we completely miss the spiritual dimension. We would then qualify for the description 'carnal Christian.' In this case it is rather like having a hard shell forming around the human spirit. Whilst the person is born again, the Spirit is having a limited effect in their lives because the flesh (the body and soul) is being allowed to dominate."[2]

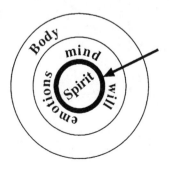

Hardened shell—
spirit has little influence

The person is still born again, even if backsliding or deliberately sinning, but is grieving the Holy Spirit living within him, and is not living in the way God intended, in the joy and peace resulting from fellowship with Him.

As we pray in the Spirit (i.e. in tongues), we build up our spirit man (Jude 20). He who speaks in a tongue edifies himself (1 Corinthians 14:4); that is, he builds his spirit man so that it takes ascendancy over the body and soul. We do not have new bodies or new souls. Although we are no more 'slaves to sin' (Romans 6:6), we may still be servants of sin in our bodies and souls. We are born again as 'baby' Christians and we have to bring our bodies into submission to our new spirits and renew our minds according to the word. This is the process of becoming mature. We must stop being dominated by our bodies and our emotions; we must stop being mind-led. We must learn to be Spirit-led, then as we learn to walk in the Spirit we will not fulfil the desires of the flesh (see Galatians 5:16).

Filled with the fullness of the Holy Spirit. (Baptised in the Spirit)

When we are baptised in the Spirit (Matthew 3:11, Acts 1:5, 8, Acts 2:1–4), we become filled with the fullness of the Holy Spirit and empowered for witness. 'It is so much easier for our souls and our bodies to flow with the leadings and promptings of the Holy Spirit when they are also filled with His presence.' [3]

[1] *Inherent Power* Peter Michell, ICCC 1997. Used by permission
[2] Ibid.
[3] Op. cit. p.22

Chapter Three

WHAT FAITH IS

So then faith comes by hearing, and hearing by the word of God.
Romans 10:17

Hebrews 11:6 tells us that it is impossible to please God without faith. It is therefore very important to understand what faith is, and to learn to walk by faith. Faith is overcoming the natural mind to believe God's word, despite any evidence or circumstances to the contrary. The world's view has always been 'seeing is believing', but for the Christian, 'believing is seeing.' 'Now faith is the substance of things hoped for, the evidence of things not seen' (Hebrews 11:1). Faith has always to be exercised before we see the result, because faith is in the present, and is an expectation of something in the future. It has nothing to do with what we see or feel or hear, but only with what God's word says. Here it is important that we distinguish between the *logos* word and the *rhema* word. We cannot stand in faith on the logos, only on the rhema word which we have received and which has become alive in our hearts.

When God spoke to Noah and told him to build an ark, Noah was divinely warned of things not yet seen (Hebrews 11:7). In other words, God spoke to him personally, and Noah believed and acted on God's word (v.22). He believed and responded to the word although he lived far inland and, it would seem, there was a severe drought at the time. This is the kind of faith God wants us to have— faith which is based on God's word despite any contrary circumstances; faith which doesn't waver, in Noah's case for one hundred and twenty years; faith which results in obedience to the word. Faith requires corresponding action.

Demonstrating to his disciples the kind of faith God requires, when he cursed the fig tree (Mark 11:12–14, 20–24), Jesus said,

19

"Whoever says to this mountain... and does not doubt in his heart, but believes that those things he says will be done...." Here we have three important elements of faith. Firstly, it is in the heart, not in the mind. Secondly, it cannot exist together with doubt; doubt negates faith. Thirdly, the faith in the heart must be spoken out of the mouth. When you can say what God says, your words become creative. Wesley spoke of the greatest problem in the church of his day as being that of mental assent. We have the same problem today. The mind is influenced by logic and experience, but the spirit (the heart) receives and acts on the word of God. The mind receives the logos by natural intellect; the heart (spirit) receives the *rhema* by supernatural means, through the Holy Spirit. The word in our minds brings mental assent, but the word in our heart brings faith. The word must go from our minds into our hearts for it to produce faith.

Some time ago, while on holiday in Bali, I had the opportunity to do something I had long wanted to try. We were standing on a beach, from which people were parasailing. However, it is one thing to want to try it when there is no opportunity, but quite a different matter when there is nothing to stop you! I watched people taking off and landing without any problem. I must have watched this at least twenty times, and the man selling it explained carefully to me how safe it was. In my head I knew it was quite safe, but there was a little voice telling me that it was not covered by my holiday insurance! Eventually I was convinced by his words, and was strapped into the harness. Takeoff was simple. There was none of the wild flapping, like a demented seagull trying to get off the ground, that I had envisaged! Landing was equally easy, and I wondered then what I had worried about. These people knew what they were doing and I could trust them. It was certainly a wonderful experience, and one that I have since repeated several times. Do you see the difference? Whilst I had the mental assent in my mind that it was obviously safe, I was still swayed by doubts and fears. It was only when I was convinced in my heart that I was prepared to act in accordance with my belief. In the same way, when God tells us to do something, we must learn to ignore the little voice whispering to us that it won't work or that we shall just look foolish. We must trust that God will do what He says.

The people of Israel were in this position. God had told them to enter the land of Canaan, which He was going to give them. He had promised this land to them, in the covenant made to their forefather Abraham. It was a good land, full of mineral resources, fruit and water. All they had to do was go in and take it, but when the spies that were sent in to spy out the land returned, ten of the twelve gave a negative report. They spoke in fear, saying that the cities were heavily fortified and the people were giants. They looked at the circumstances rather than believing the promise of God. Only Joshua and Caleb spoke in faith, with Caleb saying, "Let us go up at once and take possession, for we are well able to overcome it" (Numbers 13:30b). Because of their doubt and fear and disobedience, the Israelites wandered in the wilderness for forty years, until all that generation had died, and only Joshua and Caleb entered the promised land. It is, of course, important to recognise the facts. The cities were heavily fortified, with walls six feet wide and twenty-five to thirty feet high. The people living there were giants. This is borne out by the discovery in 1918, by Gustav Dalman, of great basalt graves, dolmen, on the old site of Rabbath-Ammon, corresponding in size to the dimensions given for Og, the giant king of Bashan. Subsequently, it has been found that graves such as these are common in Palestine. Years later, David defeated one of their descendants, the Philistine Goliath, by trusting in God. We should not deny the facts, but believe that God is able to change or overcome them according to His promise. We need to speak in line with His promised outcome.

The account of the Israelites' failure to enter the promised land of Canaan, given in chapter three of the Epistle to the Hebrews, explains why they were unable to go up and possess the land. It was because of 'an evil heart of unbelief.' Just as faith is in the heart, so unbelief, the opposite of faith, is in the heart. Chapter four of Hebrews tells us that 'the word which they heard did not profit them, not being mixed with faith.' Hebrews 3:10 gives the reason they were not able to have faith in their hearts. It was because 'they always go astray in their hearts, and they have not known My ways.' In Psalm 103:7, we read that God, '...made known His ways to Moses, His acts to the children of Israel.' This, then, is why Moses trusted God. He sought God's face; the people sought His provision. Exodus 33:13,18 tells us that Moses asked God to teach him His ways so that he would know Him; and to show him His glory. It is when we seek to know God for *who He is* rather than *what He can do for us*, that we really know Him and trust Him. Hebrews 11:6 tells us that 'He is a rewarder of those who diligently seek Him.'

Sadly, the Israelites compounded their problems once they realised their mistake, by trying to enter the land when God had not given them a word to do so. In fact, Moses told them that the Lord would not go with them, yet they acted presumptuously, went into the land, and were thereupon defeated by the Amorites. It is so important only to move on a word from the Lord and then only at the time He gives it. We cannot make a word given to other people or for another time apply whenever or however we would like.

There is only one way by which faith comes, and that is by hearing the word of God. (See Romans 10:17.) This is not a 'one-off' event, but it is by continuously hearing the word. Then, when we have received the *rhema* word of God **we need to speak it**. Abraham provides a good example of how to live by faith. After having heard the promise that he would bear a son, he did not consider the circumstances of his great age, nor that of his wife Sarah, who was naturally past being able to conceive. Instead, he believed God. However, we see the danger of trying to 'help God along!' Sarah's idea of giving her maid Hagar to him to bear him a son was not what God had said. Abraham was eighty six when Hagar's son Ishmael was born. This caused problems of rivalry and jealousy for Sarah, Hagar and Ishmael, and divided loyalty for Abraham. Eventually, Sarah made Abraham drive Hagar and her son out of the house. Thirteen years later, God reaffirmed His promise to Abraham that he would have a child and that it would be Sarah, his wife who would bear the child. Then, a year later, Sarah produced Isaac, and Genesis 21:1–2 tells us that 'the Lord did for Sarah as He had spoken', and that she bore Abraham a son in his old age, 'at the set time of which God had spoken to him.' God always does what He has promised, but it requires faith and patience to wait for the fulfilment in *His* time. We read in Romans chapter four that, in all that time of waiting, Abraham did not waver through unbelief, because he knew his God and knew that He would do what He had said. During this time he: 'was strengthened in faith, giving glory to God' (Romans 4:20). The secret of not wavering is praise. Even when God asked Abraham to sacrifice Isaac, Abraham knew that God had promised seed like the stars and the sand from Isaac, and so he believed that God would even be able to raise Isaac up from the dead, for he knew that God's word could be trusted.

When the woman with the haemorrhage of blood came to Jesus to be healed (Mark 5:25–31) we read first of all that she heard about Jesus, then she came and touched his garment and she said, 'if only I may touch His clothes, I shall be made well.' Her faith came from hearing, she believed and acted in accordance with her belief, and she spoke her expectation out of her mouth. In 2 Corinthians 4:13, Paul tells us, '...since we have the same spirit of faith, according to what is written, "I believe and therefore I speak"....' We must be careful that what we speak out of our mouths are faith-filled words. Words can either build up faith or destroy faith.

The Bible tells us no fewer than four times that **the right-eous shall live by faith**. It must be a way of life for us. In order to be able to do this, we must know our God, know His word, learn to listen to His voice and be obedient to it. Jesus said that man shall not live by bread alone, but by every word which proceeds from the mouth of God. In other words, by every *rhema* word of God. If we are to live by faith and to live by the word, it follows that we must live by faith in the word of God. Only when we have received the rhema word, and it is living in our hearts, can we act on it. Our faith will grow as we learn to walk in the word.

Chapter Four

NEW CREATION REALITIES

*Therefore, if anyone is in Christ, he is a new creation; old
things have passed away; behold, all things have become new.*

2 Corinthians 5:17

What does it mean to be a new creation? The part of us that has
become new, when we receive Jesus into our lives, is the spirit. Our
bodies and our souls are still the same. However, the spirit has been
born again, as Jesus explained to Nicodemus (John 3:3-6). Romans
8:10 says, 'And if Christ is in you, the body is dead because of sin,
but the Spirit is life because of righteousness.' This new spirit is
righteous because God tells us that we receive righteousness as a
gift by faith in Jesus. (See Philippians 3:9). This is the only way we
can become righteous. No matter how good a life we lead, we can
never meet God's standard of righteousness ourselves, (Ephesians
2:8). Jesus, by his death and resurrection, gives us his righteousness. (See 1 Corinthians 1:30 and 2 Corinthians 5:21).

Being righteous means that we have the ability to stand in the
presence of the Father God as though we had never sinned, and
without any sense of guilt or inferiority (Romans 8:1). We have
been declared not guilty. We will never become more righteous.
We cannot grow in righteousness, as our righteousness in Christ is
complete. However, we can grow in *awareness* of our righteousness. E.W Kenyon has said, 'Sin consciousness has robbed man of
faith and filled him with a sense of unworthiness.' From the time
Adam and Eve sinned, they became aware of their unrighteousness
and tried to hide from God. They had lost their covering of glory
and realised they were naked. Jesus has made it possible for man to
be restored to the state he was in before the fall, so now man can
again approach God without fear. We have been given restored fel-

lowship with the Father. In Christ Jesus we have been made acceptable to God. (Ephesians 1:5,6). We have been adopted into God's family as His children and made joint heirs with Jesus. (Romans 8:15–17).

Of course, being declared righteous does not mean that we can just carry on sinning. We will inevitably sin, because our souls and bodies have not been changed. But, although our righteousness does not depend on our not sinning, we no longer delight in sinning (see Romans 6:1,2). We now want to live the life of righteousness—doing the works of righteousness, and bearing the fruit of righteousness.

Chapter Five

FAITH & HOPE

Now faith is the substance of things hoped
for, the evidence of things not seen.   Hebrews 11:1

Since the Epistle to the Hebrews declares that 'faith is the substance of things hoped for, the evidence of things not seen' (11:1), it is obvious that hope is an essential part of faith. We tend to use the word 'hope' in a rather negative way. We say things like, 'I hope it won't rain tomorrow', meaning that we expect it will; or, 'I hope I have passed my exam', thinking, 'but I don't think I have.' Sometimes, when you ask a person whether he believes God can heal him, he may say 'I hope so.' This suggests, 'I'd like to think so, but I doubt if it will happen.' The Concise Oxford Dictionary suggests a very different meaning. It defines hope as 'expectation and desire combined'. The Greek word used in Hebrews, *elpis*, means to anticipate, usually with pleasure — a favourable, confident expectation. Hope involves trust, expectation and desire.

Hope is necessary for faith to work on. Hope is the goal setter which faith brings into reality. Hope is the vision, which faith sets out to accomplish. Nothing is achieved without it first being conceived as a hope-picture. Everything begins as an idea or vision of the future, and faith brings it into the present. Walt Disney died before Disneyland in Florida was opened. At the opening ceremony, one of his friends remarked, 'I wish Walt could have seen this.' His wife replied, 'He did.' Without hope there is nothing but despair. The most important thing we can give people is hope.

There must always be a reason for hope. Peter tells us we should always be ready to give a reason for the hope we have been given of eternal life (1 Peter 3:15). Natural hope is based on experience, but supernatural hope is based on God's rhema word. Our faith, therefore, will never exceed our knowledge of the word. We need to study and meditate on the word, in order to build that hope-picture. Then, because hope is in the future, there is a time of waiting for the fulfilment of the word. During this time, it is important to keep our eyes fixed on that hope-picture. Hebrews 6:17–19 describes how this inner image of hope is the thing which holds our soul, i.e. our mind and emotions, from wavering, even if circumstances seem to be pointing in a contrary direction.

The example of Abraham gives us a picture of how we are to wait in hope. Firstly, when all natural hope was gone, he continued to base his hope on God's promise to him. He did not consider the circumstances of his great age, nor that of his wife, Sarah. Instead, holding on firmly to the promise, he held his mind and emotions in line with the word. He discovered the secret of praise; giving glory to God strengthened his faith, enabling him to concentrate on the faithfulness of the promise-maker, rather than the circumstances.

George Muller, the founder of the Muller Children's Homes, had a vision for building an orphanage, but there was no money to do so. He found a site, where he believed God wanted him to build, marking it with two sticks. Then the money started coming in. Often there was no money for food, but he would sit down at the table with the children and give thanks for the meal. There would be a knock on the door and someone standing there with food!

The evangelist Reinhard Bonnke had a vision for a 'blood-washed Africa'. He 'saw' thousands turning to Christ. Today, there are only very few countries in Africa where he has not held meetings. As he preaches throughout the continent, millions of people hear the gospel message through his ministry. God is the source of our hope. His word provides the vision. Once the vision of hope is established in our hearts by meditation on the word, we can rest in that hope, and wait patiently for its fulfilment.

Chapter Six

RENEWING THE MIND

*And do not be conformed to this world, but be transformed by the
renewing of your mind, that you may prove what is that good and
acceptable and perfect will of God.*   Romans 12:2

Ephesians 1:4 tells us that God intends us to be 'holy and without
blame before Him in love.' God intends that we should be made
like Jesus, as we learn from Romans 8:29: 'For whom He foreknew,
He also predestined to be conformed to the image of His Son....'
This can only come about as we reckon ourselves dead to the flesh,
but alive to the Spirit. Paul says, 'I have been crucified with Christ;
it is no longer I who live, but Christ lives in me; and the life which
I now live in the flesh I live by faith in the Son of God, who loved
me and gave Himself for me' (Galatians 2:20). That this is a process, in which we choose to allow our renewed spirits to dominate
over our bodies and souls, is made clear in 2 Corinthians 3:18: 'But
we all, with unveiled face, beholding as in a mirror the glory of the
Lord, are being transformed into the same image from glory to glory,
just as by the Spirit of the Lord.' It is vital that we understand the
nature of this active, positive process of transformation, and Paul,
in his letter to the Romans, shows us what a radical change from
our former alignment with worldly thinking is involved: 'I beseech
you therefore, brethren, by the mercies of God, that you present
your bodies a living sacrifice, holy, acceptable to God, which is
your reasonable service. And do not be conformed to this world,
but be transformed by the renewing of your mind, that you may
prove what is that good and acceptable and perfect will of God'
(Romans 12:1,2). **Do not be conformed to this world**. How? By
being transformed by the renewing of the mind. 'Renewing' means
changing our way of thinking. The Greek word for 'transformed' is

from the same root as our 'metamorphosis'—a word that signifies a change in form. Consider the tadpole. It metamorphoses into a frog. Whilst remaining the same individual, still with the same genetic make-up or constitution, the adult frog bears little resemblance to the tadpole, and its way of life has been totally changed. The metamorphosis from tadpole to frog is not instant, but is a process which takes several weeks. Essentially, it involves the switching off of some genes and the switching on of others. This results in the gradual process of loss of tail, growth of limbs, change from external gills to internal gills and thence to lungs, a change in the digestive system (even what it feeds on changes!) and a change in the texture and colour of the skin. In other words, some things associated with life in the pond have to go, and new structures associated with life on land develop. Do you see the similarity? When we are born again, there is an initial change by which our spirits are made new. Then God has, 'delivered us from the power of darkness and conveyed us into the kingdom of the Son of His love' (Colossians 1:13). However, this is only the start of the changes in our lives. At this stage there is no outward difference. We then have to go through the process of sanctification, which is analogous to the biological process of metamorphosis experienced by the tadpole. During this process, old things associated with the old way of life have to go and new things must become part of us. This is emphasised in Ephesians 4:22–24, '..that you put off, concerning your former conduct, the old man which grows corrupt according to the deceitful lusts, and be renewed in the spirit of your mind, and that you put on the new man which was created according to God, in true righteousness and holiness.' In the tadpole, these changes come about by the release of hormones and enzymes, which alter the nature of the cells. In Christians, the changes come about by the release of the Holy Spirit and by saturating our minds with the word of God, which alters our thinking. We learn to be led by the Spirit rather than the mind.

Renewing our minds is achieved by meditating on the word of God. Then we establish new thought patterns that are based on His word. It is by allowing the word to become implanted into us that our minds, wills and emotions (our souls) will be saved. (See James 1:21). When we became born again, our spirits were saved and made holy, but our souls and bodies were not saved by faith; they have to be renewed and brought into submission to our renewed spirit. (See Galatians 5:16). As we choose to walk according to the Spirit, we shall not have the same desires of the fleshly man. How do we learn to walk in the Spirit? It is by allowing God's words to abide in us. (See John 15:7). Jesus tells his disciples to *continue* in his word. (See John 8:31). Continual feeding on the word of God will renew the mind, bringing it into line with the renewed spirit. The result is that God's desires will be our desires.

Jesus tells us that where our treasure is— that is where our hearts will be. (See Matthew 6:21). In other words, it is what we value that determines our thinking. We must set our minds on things of the Spirit if we are to become like Jesus. (See Romans 8:5,6,8). It is sometimes said that, 'we are what we eat', but the Bible teaches us that we are what we meditate on.

Chapter Seven

FAITH AND PATIENCE

'...do not become sluggish, but imitate those who
through faith and patience inherit the promises.'
Hebrews 6:12

Patience is an integral part of faith. Since faith is exercised for something which we do not yet have or see, it is necessary to wait for it with patience. Patience is the possessing power of faith, enabling us not to waver. Just as faith without love does not work, because faith works by love (see Galatians 5:6), so faith without patience will not stand firm on God's word in the face of contradiction from Satan. During the waiting time, Satan will try to get us to doubt. Patience is about learning to control our thoughts. Luke 21:19 instructs us, 'By your patience possess your souls.' If we obey this command and exercise patience, we will be in control of our thoughts and emotions; they will not run riot and torment us. In 1 Thessalonians 1:2-3, Paul says, 'We give thanks to God always for you all... remembering without ceasing your work of faith, labour of love, and patience of hope in our Lord Jesus Christ....' And he includes patience as one of the things that are 'proper for sound doctrine.' (See Titus 2:1–2)

Anything worth having is worth waiting for. Hebrews 6:12 tells us not to become lazy, and declares that the promises of God are inherited through faith and patience. However, patience does not come easily to most of us; it must be learnt. We can wait patiently for the promise of someone we trust. Trust is developed by knowing the person. Gained through personal knowledge of God, trust has the confidence to wait patiently for His time to answer. Our knowledge of God is developed as we study His word and spend time with Him in prayer.

31

It is a common misconception that tribulation and testing come to increase our faith. However, the Bible tells us that faith comes by hearing the word of God, and that tribulation produces *patience*, not faith. The testing of our faith produces patience which leads to maturity (James 1:4). It is for this reason that we are to 'count it all joy' when we have tribulations.

David learned the secret of waiting on the Lord, as we see in Psalm 27:14, 'Wait on the LORD; Be of good courage, and He shall strengthen your heart; Wait, I say, on the LORD.' This shows us that he encouraged himself by waiting on the Lord in prayer and meditation. In Psalm 62:5, David says, 'My soul, wait silently for God alone, For my expectation is from Him.'

In contrast, the Israelites constantly made a mess of things because of their lack of patience. Psalm 106:13 tells us, 'They soon forgot His works; They did not wait for His counsel....' or, ' They did not wait for His plans to develop respecting them' [AMP].

Waiting forces the flesh (i.e. that in us which opposes God) to die, teaching us to persevere with confident hope in God's promises. 'The LORD is good to those who wait for Him, To the soul who seeks Him. It is good that one should hope and wait quietly for the salvation of the Lord' (Lamentations 3:25–26). Meanwhile, the hearts of those around you may be revealed. Exercise discernment regarding other people and what they are saying to you, not allowing negative comments to weaken your hold on the promises of God. Also, the Lord takes time to train you for spiritual warfare. 'Blessed be the Lord my Rock, who trains my hands for war' (Psalm 144:1). The time of waiting may itself be where a spiritual battle is fought, as the Lord gives you an opportunity to come into deeper dependence upon Him. The sort of Christian that God wants you to be is one who endures without losing trust and hope in what your heavenly Father has promised you. It has been observed that waiting times allow God to deal with an obstacle in a miraculous way. If we are awaiting the resolution of a problem or difficulty, it is important not to try to run ahead of God. He may need to change some circumstance before a vision or promise can be fulfilled.

Chapter Eight

THE POWER OF THE TONGUE

Death and life are in the power of the tongue,
And those who love it will eat its fruit.

Proverbs 18:21

When a dear Christian friend said to me, 'My feet are killing me', she was surprised as I gently pointed out that speaking these words gave Satan an opportunity in her life. Maybe this sounds a bit dramatic or superstitious to you. This is a common enough saying, but I hope to show you in this study how Satan, who has no creative power of his own, will try to get us to say things which he can use against us.

There are so many things like this that people say. 'I was worried to death; you'll be the death of me; I am dying for a drink; he'll never amount to much; she's a worrier just like her mother', and so on. Parents may be heard to say such things as, 'Here comes trouble', as their child approaches. As a teacher, I often heard students say, 'I'll never pass this exam.' I clearly remember a time when things were difficult, and I found myself saying, 'I can't cope'.

All these things are contrary to what the word of God says. The word says, 'With long life will I satisfy you.' 'Cast all your cares on him.' 'I can do all things through Christ who strengthens me'. Jesus clearly taught in John 10:10, 'The thief does not come except to steal, and to kill and to destroy. I have come that they may have life, and that they may have it more abundantly.' By stating these negatives we are agreeing with Satan, who comes to kill, steal and destroy. **We are effectively speaking curses over ourselves.**

The word puts it very clearly in Proverbs 18:21, 'Death and life are in the power of the tongue, and those who love it will eat its fruit.' Or, as the amplified version puts it, 'Death and life are in the power of the tongue and they who indulge it shall eat the fruit of it' (death or life). [AMP] Similarly, Proverbs 13:3 [AMP] 'He who guards his mouth keeps his life, but he who opens wide his lips [i.e. with foolish talk] will come to destruction.' This does not, of course, mean that the minute we say something foolish, Satan will immediately come in and bring it upon us, but we are giving him the legal right, and he may use our words against us at some point. The concept of law is appropriate at this point, because the laws of God are contained in His word. Disobedience to God's law can open us up to the attacks of the enemy. We have the choice as to whether we speak the life-filled words of God or the destructive words of Satan. Jesus said, 'the words that I speak to you are spirit, and they are life' (John 6:63b).

Words are a creative force. This was so from the beginning of the world. It was the spoken word of God which created the world. 'Then God said, "Let there be light; and there was light"' (Genesis 1:3.) In Genesis 1:6–7, God says, 'Let there be a firmament in the midst of the waters....and it was so.' And again, in verses 9,11,14–15, 20–24, 26–30, we have the pattern 'God said... and it was so.' Hebrews 11:3 tells us, 'By faith we understand that the worlds were framed by the word of God....' Out of chaos God brought forth order and life by the words of His mouth. We are given in the Scriptures this remarkable picture of God creating with His mouth, imagery that teaches us the vital significance of divine speech and communication. Having created the world, we read that Jesus sustains it by his word. In Hebrews 1:3 he is said to be, '....upholding all things by the word of his power....' Let us note that it is the word of his power, not the power of his word. This means that the word is the vehicle which carries his power.

Dick Mills tells a lovely story, which illustrates this point well. He was about to go on holiday, when a friend telephoned to say that his wife had been taken into hospital with a severe heart attack. He asked Dick to go and pray for her. Dick and his wife went to the hospital but, as the woman was seriously ill, only Dick was allowed to go in to see her. Dick's wife was taken by the ward sister to wait in the room where all the monitors were. Before leaving the room, the nursing sister warned Dick not to upset the woman. After a moment or two of praying, Dick spoke out verses from psalms: 'Wait on the LORD; Be of good courage and He shall strengthen your heart' (Psalm 27:14); 'Be of good courage, And He shall strengthen your heart, All you who hope in the LORD (Psalm 31:24). At that point, the nursing sister arrived, saying, 'I told you not to excite her.' Back in the car, he asked his wife what the sister had been so upset about. His wife explained that, every time Dick had spoken the word of God, a surge of power had registered on the heart monitor. Within a week, the woman was out of hospital. **The word of God spoken in faith carries power**. The psalmist says, 'He sent His word and healed them...' (Psalm107:20).

Jesus' word had creative power. We see this in the incident in Matthew 8:8, in which the centurion came to ask the Lord to heal his servant, saying, 'only speak a word, and my servant will be healed.' In verse 13 we read, 'Then Jesus said to the centurion, "Go your way; and as you have believed, so let it be done for you." And his servant was healed that same hour.' Jesus also spoke to the storm on the Lake of Galilee, saying: "Peace, be still!" The result was that, 'the wind ceased and there was great calm' (Mark 4:39). In Matthew 8:27, we read how they marvelled that even the winds and the sea obeyed Jesus. When Jesus went to the tomb of Lazarus, three days after he had died, he cried out 'Lazarus, come forth!' and Lazarus came out of the tomb. (See John 11:43,44.) Jesus' word gave life. By his word, then, the authority and power of God was brought to bear over nature, death and life.

Jesus taught his disciples the importance of the spoken word, when he cursed the fig tree. This was an object lesson for them. When Jesus saw that the fig tree had no fruit, he said to it, 'Let no one eat fruit from you ever again'(Mark 11:14). Subsequently, when they were passing by, they saw that the fig tree had dried up from the roots. Jesus explains to the disciples that their words could carry the same power. 'Assuredly, I say to you, if you have faith and do not doubt, you will not only do what was done to the fig tree, but also if you say to this mountain, "Be removed and be cast into the sea," it will be done' (Matthew 21:21).

From the teaching of Jesus, we learn that we shall have whatever we say, if we ask in true faith. This is because man was made in God's image, so man's words, similarly, have creative potential. When the word of God is believed in the heart and spoken with the mouth, the Holy Spirit brings to life that spoken word. In Jeremiah 1:12, the Lord God says: 'I am ready to perform My word.' **We must learn to speak positively in line with the word of God into our situations and over our families**. This is the principle of speaking blessings over people and circumstances.

However, negative words will give Satan the legal right to bring his evil against us. He has no creative power of his own. Instead, he tries to deceive us into using our tongues to accomplish his purposes. Ecclesiastes 10:8 says, 'He who digs a pit will fall into it, And whoever breaks through a wall will be bitten by a serpent.' Negative speech is one of the main ways in which we break down our wall of protection, so allowing Satan to attack us. James 3:1-12 accurately describes the difficulty we have in controlling our tongues, and the devastation which an unruly tongue can cause.

Friends of ours had been married for three years, but were unable to conceive a baby. After time spent with their pastor in prayer, the Lord reminded Ann that, before she had been married, she had said, 'I never want a baby'. These words had acted like a curse on her. Once they were broken, she conceived— the very next month!

When we first met Jean, she wore a neck support, and was frequently in a wheelchair. She had had prayer and received a measure of healing, but was not completely restored. After hearing a talk about the power of the tongue, she asked the Lord to show her anything that might be causing her illness. He reminded her that when her son was very young he had a disease, which had identical symptoms. She had said, 'Lord, if you will heal him, I will take the illness, but please wait until the children are old enough to manage.' God had healed the child, but Satan had put the sickness on her when the children grew up. We prayed, and broke the power of the word she had spoken. To quote her own words, she has 'never looked back', and she no longer has a wheelchair.

Recently, we met a vicar who had suffered with ME for two years. We discovered that he had been overworked, and had said in desperation, 'I wouldn't mind having ME for two weeks, so that I could get a rest'. As my husband says, 'Why didn't he say, "I would love a two week holiday in Barbados?"' The curse was broken, and he is now well.

In Proverbs 6:2, we read, 'You are snared by the words of your mouth; you are taken by the words of your mouth.' However, we can bind the power of words and curses spoken over us, and release God's word, which will then work in our lives.

The spirit world is controlled by the word of God. The natural world is to be controlled by man speaking God's word. We considered earlier Jesus' teaching on faith in Mark 11:23, "Whoever... does not doubt in his heart, but believes that those things he says will be done, he will have whatever he says." Note the condition. There are always conditions to God's promises. It is only if we do not doubt in our heart that we shall have what we say. We have to believe in our hearts, not our heads—and then speak it with our mouths. In other words, theoretical belief is insufficient. In Luke 17:6, Jesus says, "If you have faith as a mustard seed, you can say to this mulberry tree, 'Be pulled up by the roots and be planted in the sea,' and it would obey you." Thus, faith is released by the words of our mouths. Again, in 2 Corinthians 4:13, we read, 'And since we have the same spirit of faith, according to what is written, "I believed and therefore I spoke," we also believe and therefore speak.' God's word conceived in your heart, formed by the tongue, and spoken out of your own mouth, becomes a spiritual force releasing the ability of God within you. It has been said, 'if you don't like what is happening to you, change what you are speaking.' This is not a magic formula, nor is it superstition: it is a Biblical principle. **'For out of the abundance of the heart the mouth speaks. A good man out of the good treasure of his heart brings forth good things, and an evil man out of the evil treasure brings forth evil things. But I say to you that for every idle word men may speak, they will give account of it in the day of judgment. For by your words you will be justified and by your words you will be condemned'** (Matthew 12:34b–37). This is the spiritual law of 'each reproducing after its own kind'. So we must be sure to fill our hearts with the good treasure of the word of God, so that this is what comes out of our mouth, even when under pressure—rather than the negative things which Satan wants us to say. We shall have to give an account for all the foolish words which we speak. We must programme our hearts by meditating on the word; we need to establish it in our hearts by speaking it to ourselves. James 1:21 says, '...and receive with meekness the implanted word, which is able to save your souls.' [Meekness meaning here, having a teachable spirit]. He is not talking here about being born again, but about the word becoming so much part of us that we live according to the word, and so have peace and success in the soul (mind, will and emotions). In Proverbs16:23, we are taught that, 'The heart of the wise teaches his mouth....' As we begin to speak according to the word of God, in obedience and faith, we discover that the Lord brings more of His abundant blessings. He wants to give health, wisdom and success to us and our families. (See Proverbs 4:20–27). Speaking the word of God, and refraining from 'idle words' that give the enemy a foothold, is a vital aspect of growing in Christian maturity.

Chapter Nine

DOUBT AND FEAR:
THE ENEMIES OF FAITH

Be anxious for nothing, but in everything by prayer
and supplication, with thanksgiving, let your requests
be made known to God; and the peace of God, which
surpasses all understanding, will guard your hearts
and minds through Christ Jesus.

Philippians 4:6,7

Doubt and fear are Satan's two main weapons. Fear is the expectation of the worst; it results from confessing Satan's negatives. It has been said that fear is caused by going into dark places and developing your negatives! It is the opposite of faith, which results from confessing God's word. Fear destroys faith.

The chief thing that Satan wants us to do is to doubt the goodness of God, for it is the goodness of God that leads man to repentance. (See Romans 2:4.) Satan would like us to believe that any bad things that happen are the will of God. This is contrary to all that the Bible says, but is often dressed up to sound religious. How often one hears someone say, 'Why does God allow it?' when in fact it has been the work of the devil, and man has allowed it, either deliberately or inadvertently. If we know the word of God, we know that God is good, and that everything He does is good. (Again, see John 10:10).

Satan also wants us to doubt the word of God. Doubt questions the integrity of His word. Doubt has its roots in rebellion to the spoken word of God. Right from the beginning, Satan encouraged man to question what God had said. "Has God indeed said, 'You shall not eat of every tree of the garden'?" Satan falsely affirms,'You will not surely die.' (See Genesis 3:1–4). We see the

39

result in verse 10, when Adam answers God, saying, 'I was afraid....'

The Greek word for doubt means 'standing in two ways'. It means wavering between hope and fear. The epistle of James teaches us that a person who doubts will not receive anything from the Lord. (See James 1:6–7). We need to take control of our thoughts, and learn to recognise where they are coming from. When my husband Don goes out preaching, he frequently returns late at night, sometimes in the early hours of the morning. I used to go to bed and wait for him. Sometimes, unable to sleep, I would get up and pace about, imagining him having gone to sleep at the wheel of the car, and being upside down in a ditch! It was only when I learnt to recognise that these thoughts were being put in my mind by Satan, and therefore were lies, that I was able to pray for God's protection for him— and then trust that he would be safe. We had friends who used to say, 'Why pray, when you can worry!' How many of us do just that... pray, and then continue to worry? Paul says, 'Be anxious for nothing, but in everything by prayer and supplication, with thanksgiving, let your requests be made known to God....' With this attitude we discover that, '...the peace of God, which surpasses all understanding, will guard your hearts and minds through Christ Jesus' (Philippians 4:6,7). Worry and anxiety all too easily take root in our minds and hearts, if we permit them to do so, but the peace of God will guard us against it—when we pray and trust in the Lord.

The phrase 'Do not fear' appears 365 times in the Bible; once for each day of the year! Fear is the expectation of the worst; it is faith in the devil. It is a self-fulfilling prophecy. Job said, 'For the thing I greatly feared has come upon me, And what I dreaded has happened to me' (Job 3:25). Fear is the opposite of faith. Jesus said to the disciples, in the boat after the storm, 'Why are you fearful, O you of little faith?' (Matthew 8:26). Here he was using a word which meant underdeveloped faith; faith not developed in God's word.

The antidote to fear is knowing the Father's love. 'There is no fear in love; but perfect love casts out fear...' (1 John 4:18). The Holy Spirit brings us into that close relationship and knowledge of God as *Abba*, Father. This word, *Abba*, used by Jesus, is the word by which children speak to their fathers, suggesting unreasoning trust. When we know God in this way, we know His perfect love for us. As adopted children of the heavenly Father, we have no need to fear. The words of the psalmist can be our own: 'I am like a green olive tree, in the house of God; I trust in the mercy of God for ever and ever (Psalm 52:8). That this is a gift to Christians, that we can receive and enjoy is clear: '...God has not given us a spirit of fear, but of power and of love and of a sound mind' (2 Timothy 1:7). Fear brings torment in the mind, but the knowledge of the love of God brings peace. Hebrews 13:6 reminds us of God's promise to His servant, "I will never leave you nor forsake you." Consequently, '...we may boldly say: "The LORD is my helper; I will not fear. What can man do to me?"'

A spirit of fear may enter via heredity, in which case one can be cut off from things inherited. Or a spirit of fear may have come through some experience or action, such as watching violent films or horror movies, or by involvement in some occult activity, such as seances, ouija boards, fantasy games or fortune telling. In such situations, it is necessary to repent of the involvement, renounce it, and be cut off from the effects of the experience by a prayer of deliverance. A spirit may be recognised by the fear being an irrational driving force, which may in turn have led to depression.

Not all fear is caused by spirits. Fear is a state which often results from insecurity. When fear is meditated on, it leads to anxiety and worry. It is often unsubstantiated. It may focus on some 'worst case scenario'— concerning something which, in reality, never happens. Worriers live in the future, saying, 'What if...?' By learning to live a day at a time, trusting in the love of our heavenly Father, we begin to realise that our fears are unfounded. Jesus tells us not to worry about our lives, because our Father knows our needs. (See Luke 12:22–30). When we keep our minds focused on God, He will keep us in peace. 'You will keep him in perfect peace, Whose mind is stayed on You, Because he trusts in You' (Isaiah 26:3). The more we meditate on the verses which remind us of God's faithfulness, the less chance Satan has of implanting his doubts and fears in our hearts.

Chapter Ten

UNDERSTANDING AUTHORITY

"Most assuredly, I say to you, he who believes in Me, the works that I do he will do also; and greater works than these he will do, because I go to My Father."   John 14:12

There is often much confusion amongst Christians about God's sovereignty, with the result that God often gets the blame for things which He did not do or cause. Of course it is true that God's authority is sovereign. It is the highest, supreme authority and extends over all. 1 Timothy 6:15 states that He is the only Potentate (or Sovereign), and Psalm 145:13, that His Kingdom is everlasting. However, from this position of absolute sovereignty, God is legally bound by His word, for He cannot lie, and He has revealed His will in His word. He has chosen to delegate authority on earth to man. God does not override man's will; rather He has given man free will, to choose to do right or wrong. Thus, much of what happens on earth, far from being God's will, is in fact man's will, exercised disobediently, in ways that are contrary to God's purposes. In the garden of Eden, Satan persuaded Adam and Eve to disobey God's will, and to eat the forbidden fruit, leading them to believe that this would make them like God, able to choose for themselves what is good and what is evil. This remains the problem today. Mankind seeks to redefine wrongdoing, saying that it is good and making it legal, often in the guise of 'political correctness' or sometimes even under the banner of civil rights.

So it is that, by deception, Satan took the authority originally given to man. As a result of man's disobedience, the ground became cursed. (See Genesis 3:17). From then on, '...the whole world lies under the sway of the wicked one' (1 John 5:19). So it is man's actions, often instigated by Satan, that cause the suffering in this world. That this is so is obvious in the case of the suffering caused by war. We see how famine has resulted from war, in the Sudan and elsewhere. Greed and bad government can cause severe suffering, when rulers do not ensure that their country's natural resources are used to provide reasonable standards of living. The greed of some multinational companies has been blamed for disasters such as widespread pollution, and terrible flooding resulting from deforestation, because trees are no longer present to take up the water in the hills. C.S. Lewis observed that at least 80% of man's suffering had come about through bad choices made by cruel and lawless people.

The heart of God is grieved when He sees people suffer. Because of His great love for mankind, He sent Jesus to defeat Satan by His death and resurrection, and to take back the authority from him. '...For this purpose the Son of God was manifested, that He might destroy the works of the devil' (1 John 3:8). Jesus came to show us the Father, and to do His works. We read in Acts 10:38, 'how God anointed Jesus of Nazareth with the Holy Spirit and with power, who went about doing good and healing all who were oppressed by the devil, for God was with Him.' This clearly shows that it is God's will for us to be healthy, and that sickness and disease come from the devil. God has given His authority to Jesus, and in heaven God's will is done. This is why we pray that God's will shall be done on earth as it is in heaven. Jesus has delegated his authority here on earth to the believer. The authority is in the name of Jesus. In the name of Jesus we can carry out God's will on earth and do His works. (See John 14:12). Our authority as Christians is greater than the power of Satan but, unless we exercise that authority, Satan gets his way. Sometimes, what occurs is that which Satan plans and we ourselves allow. Let us be diligent to exercise our authority in a godly way, to thwart Satan's schemes.

Chapter Eleven

THE BLOOD COVENANT

Not a word failed of any good thing which the LORD had spoken to the house of Israel. All came to pass.   Joshua 21:45

A work colleague of mine had spent a year living with a tribe in Sarawak. When he gave his talks, he used to begin with 'The last time I drank blood.' He would go on to describe how he and the chief of the tribe had cut their palms and let the blood collect in a cup of pig's blood, of which each subsequently drank half. He joked about how, having entered into a blood covenant with them, he was entitled to any of their wives. Later, when he got married, I do not think it occurred to him that this was a reciprocal arrangement! Actually, a blood covenant is the most binding agreement known to man. It means that all I have is yours, and all you have is mine. It also has deep spiritual consequences.

The Mafia make covenants with each other so that they become blood brothers. The Triads also have a blood covenant ceremony. It represents total commitment to each other.

A woman pastor was telling me how, whenever her friend in the Isle of Wight asked her to call on her, she always felt she had to drop everything and go immediately, even if she didn't want to. She could never understand why, until she remembered that, as children, they had made a blood covenant. This had to be broken, in order to set her free.

In the 1870's, Stanley, searching for David Livingstone in Africa, was about to cross territory owned by a fierce warrior Chief. It was suggested that he should make a covenant with this Chief. For several days the conditions of the covenant were worked out. Cuts were made in their right legs and the blood exchanged. Vows were taken and fierce curses pronounced, should either ever break

44

the covenant. Then gifts were exchanged, to ratify the covenant. The Chief wanted Stanley's white goat and, in return, gave Stanley his own seven foot copper spear. This represented his authority. Now, Stanley and his men could pass through the territory with the protection of the authority of the Chief. They had become blood brothers.

God is a covenant God. All his dealings with men are based on His covenant. In the Old Testament we learn of the old covenant and God's dealings with Israel. In the New Testament we learn of Jesus fulfilling the old covenant on our behalf, so that we might become partakers of the new and better covenant. Unless we understand what is involved in the old covenant, we can never truly understand our position as inheritors of the new covenant.

The first covenant made by God with man was in the garden of Eden. Man was given dominion on earth by God (See Genesis 1:26–28) as long as he continued to be obedient to God's rule. Once he had disobeyed God, man brought the curse upon himself and the land. (See Genesis 3:16–19). After the flood, God made a covenant with Noah that never again would He flood the whole earth. (See Genesis 9:9–17).

There are five major covenants made between God and man: the Abrahamic covenant (Genesis 12:1–3); the Palestinian covenant (Deuteronomy 30:1–10); the Davidic covenant (2 Samuel 7:10–16), the Jeremiah covenant — anticipating the new covenant (Jeremiah 31:31–40); and the Mosaic covenant (Exodus 19:5, and Deuteronomy 28:1–68). The ultimate covenant was the new covenant, established by Jesus, in which he fulfilled all the conditions of the old covenant on our behalf.

A blood covenant involves loyalty unto death. It is an agreement made between two parties, worked out by carefully defined pledges and promises. These are perpetually binding, not only for those who make the covenant, but also for their descendants up to four generations. It symbolises a union in which all assets, debts and liabilities are held mutually; your covenant partner has a right to demand from you everything you own. It represents death to independent living: each loses his separate identity, and the life shared between them becomes the priority. Acts 17:28 says, 'for in Him we live and move and have our being.' The covenant is sealed with blood. The Hebrew word used in the old testament is *berith*, meaning to cut where blood flows. However, the word used in the new testament is the Greek word *diatheke*, which means an unequal covenant, in which one does all the giving and the other all the taking. The Abrahamic covenant, also known as the old covenant, was re-affirmed to Isaac and to Jacob, so that God became known as the God of Abraham, Isaac and Jacob. (See Leviticus 26:42 and 1 Chronicles 16:16,17).

There are several reasons why people make covenants. It may be to seal a business deal, by which the blood brothers then trade with each other, as did Stanley with the members of the African tribe. It may be to acquire protection, such as the covenant Joshua was tricked into making with the Gibeonites. This later caused problems. (See Numbers 33:55 and Joshua 23:12,13). The problems arose because God had told them not to enter into covenants or marry into any of the Canaanite nations; their covenant with God was sacred. (Exodus 34:12). However, a covenant cannot be broken and, when the Gibeonites were threatened by five kings of the Amorites, he was obliged to help them (Joshua 10:1–15). A covenant might be for love, as was the covenant made between David and Jonathan. (See 1 Samuel 18:3). It was because of this covenant that David, when he was king, asked if there were any of Jonathan's relations to whom he might show kindness. The lame Mephibosheth was brought to him, and David allowed him to live at the palace. (See 2 Samuel 9:1–13).

There were various ways of creating a covenant, but each involved the shedding of blood, either of the covenant head or his substitute, which could be another person or an animal. When cuts are made in the palms of the hands, or the wrists of the right hand (representing authority), the blood is rubbed into each others' cut, signifying that their lives have been poured out for each other and their lives have become one. Similarly, if the blood of the two is mixed and drunk, the blood has mingled and cannot be separated— again representing a united life. Often, ash was rubbed into the wound to keep it visible, and such a permanent mark in the flesh became the seal of the covenant. When Jesus became our covenant substitute, in our covenant with God, we have this exchange of lives. We give him our spiritual death, and he gives us his spiritual life. In traditional cultures, covenants could include exchanges of material elements, symbolising the person and his status; things such as weapons, coats, and rings or bracelets, representing his authority. (When Pharaoh made Joseph ruler in Egypt he gave him his ring, a fine robe and a chain, as we read in Genesis 41:41,42.) One of the most important features of covenant relationship is the right to use the covenant partner's name. Because we have the name of Jesus to use, God is our Father, and we are joint heirs with Jesus.

Marriage is a covenant, by which the identity of the individual takes on a new and distinct character — no longer is the one independent of the other. The 'two become one', vows are made, their possessions are mutually held, rings are exchanged, the one partner takes the other's name, and a meal is shared. The marriage is consummated and this may involve the shedding of blood of the female partner.

God's covenant with Israel is an eternal and unconditional covenant, depending solely on the integrity of God for its fulfilment. This covenant, also known as the covenant of strong friendship, was made with Abraham, and Abraham was subsequently known as the friend of God. (See 2 Chronicles 20:7.) Jesus said to his followers, "No longer do I call you servants... but I have called you friends" (John 15:15). Abraham would have understood the significance of the blood covenant, as such covenants were common practice amongst the Chaldeans, from whom he came. The blessings of this covenant were pronounced by God. There was the promise of future generations and a kingdom; there was the promise of land; and there was the promise of a blessing for all the nations of earth, through Abraham's seed. The promise of the great nation was reiterated in the Davidic covenant (2 Samuel 7); the promise of land was reaffirmed in the Palestinian covenant (Deuteronomy 30:1–10), and the promise of redemption by Abraham's seed was reaffirmed in the covenant recorded in Jeremiah (Jeremiah 31:31–40).

When God made the covenant with Abraham, a smoking furnace and a burning torch passed between the two halves of the animal. The smoking furnace represented God, and the burning torch foreshadowed Jesus, Abraham's seed (see Romans 15:8) , as man's representative, because God knew that Abraham could not keep the conditions of the covenant himself. God gave the 'H' of His name YHWH to Abram and to Sarai. Abram's name became Abraham, meaning father of a multitude, and Sarai became Sarah, princess of God. When He sealed the covenant, God swore by Himself; no blood was shed until Jesus sealed the covenant on the cross. Abraham circumcised himself, and subsequently every child circumcised became an inheritor of everything connected with the covenant. Thus, the covenant applied to Abraham's descendants (Genesis 17:19). As covenant head, Abraham entered into the covenant with God on behalf of his as yet unborn seed. In Galatians 3:16, we see that the promise to Abraham and his seed was fulfilled in Jesus himself, and therefore in those who are in Christ, by grace, through faith.

Having made a covenant with Abraham, God had the right to test him. The word used for 'test' actually means to prove, or to establish a fact. Because Abraham obeyed, and was prepared to sacrifice his son Isaac, he demonstrated that he would fulfil his covenant obligation. Abraham knew that, had Isaac died, God's covenant promises of descendants as numerous as the stars of heaven could not have been fulfilled (Genesis 15:5), so Abraham believed that God would even raise him from the dead (Hebrews 11:17–19), and declared to the men with them that Isaac would return with him after making the sacrifice. (See Genesis 22:5). We see a parallel here, as God was willing to sacrifice His only Son for His covenant partner. Isaac must have been in his late teens or early twenties. There was no way Abraham, by now an old man, could have sacrificed Isaac if Isaac had not been obedient to his father. Similarly, no-one could take Jesus' life from him; he was completely obedient to his Father's will. God remarks that Abraham will teach his children God's way, so that He can bring about what He had promised (Genesis 18:19). Isaac was willing to lay down his life. God then reaffirmed His covenant with Isaac. Abraham knew that God would have to provide a sacrifice (Genesis 22:8), and Jesus refers to this when he says, in John 8:56, 'Your father Abraham rejoiced to see My day, and he saw it and was glad.' Abraham saw it figuratively; he knew God would do it in reality. Jesus was the Lamb of

God. God states that the descendants of Abraham, 'shall possess the gate of their enemies' (Genesis 22:17). Jesus took the keys of death and hell.

God responded to the groaning of Israel in slavery in Egypt because of His covenant. (Exodus 6:5). The right to freedom belonged to Israel under the covenant, but they did not enjoy that freedom, because they were not aware of their covenant rights. So God made Himself known to Moses by His covenant name, 'the God of Abraham, the God of Isaac, and the God of Jacob' (Exodus 3:6). He referred to His special relationship with Israel when He said, 'Let My people go' (Exodus 5:1). He declared, 'I will bring you out.... I will rescue you.... I will redeem you.... I will take you as My people' (Exodus 6:6–7). God then proceeded to smite Egypt with plagues, until Pharaoh was willing to let Israel go. Every plague was an attack on a particular god of the Egyptians, showing that the demon powers were powerless against God. The first was an attack on the River Nile, to which the Egyptians offered sacrifices every morning, and which they worshipped as the 'father of life'. The final act of God was to bring death to the first-born. Israel was protected by the blood of the passover lamb applied to the doorposts and lintels, in obedience and faith. Once the blood was applied, the angel of death had no power. The sacrifice of a passover lamb, in which not a bone was broken, and the protection afforded by the shed blood, was a type or shadow of Jesus — the lamb of God, whose blood would be shed for us. Before they left Egypt, the Hebrews celebrated a covenant meal — the passover.

God made a covenant with Israel, known as the Mosaic covenant, in which He gave laws and rituals. But, recognising that they would not be able to keep these laws, He instituted sacrifices, to be made by the Levitical priesthood, so providing a temporary covering for the sin of the broken law. The most important of these sacrifices was to take place on the Day of Atonement, the most sacred day in Israel's calendar. Two goats were taken as a sin offering (Leviticus 16:15,22). The blood of one was to be sprinkled on the mercy seat, on the ark of the covenant in the Holy of Holies. The other, the scapegoat, was sent off into the wilderness to bear their sins, after the priest had laid his hand on its head and confessed their sins.

Here, again, we see a type of Jesus, whose blood was shed for us and who bore our sins, removing them as far as the east is from the west. (Psalm 103:12). The Mosaic covenant was to last only until the coming of the 'promised seed' Jesus, who would fulfil the conditions of the law on behalf of all who come to him in repentance and faith. The Mosaic covenant included the pronouncement of blessings, which were conditional on obedience, and curses for disobedience. While Israel kept the conditions, they had protection and blessing—health and prosperity; when they broke the covenant, they suffered defeat in battle, disease and poverty. David knew his covenant rights when he faced Goliath, to whom he referred as 'this uncircumcised Philistine' (1 Samuel 17:26). Jesus referred to the covenant when he said, 'So ought not this woman, being a daughter of Abraham, whom Satan has bound—think of it—for eighteen years, be loosed from this bond on the Sabbath?' (Luke 13:16). She was a daughter of Abraham; a daughter of the covenant, having the right to the blessing of health and healing.

Chapter Twelve

LISTENING TO GOD

My sheep hear My voice, and I know them, and they follow Me.
John 10:27

There is a hymn containing the words, 'O give me Samuel's listening ear.' For forty years, Samuel listened to God and guided the nation of Israel, but he had first to learn to recognise God's voice. God does speak to us, but so often we do not recognise His voice, or we are too busy to listen. Learning how to listen takes practice. Samuel was called three times before he recognised God's voice. John 8:47 says, 'He who is of God hears God's words,' and Jesus said, 'And when he brings out his own sheep, he goes before them; and the sheep follow him, for they know his voice.... I am the good shepherd; and I know My sheep, and am known by My own.' (John 10:4,14). The prerequisite for hearing God is that we know Him and have a close personal relationship with Him. It has nothing to do with how long we have been Christians; far more to do with how much time we spend with Him. It is the mature sheep that recognise His voice; the lambs simply follow the sheep. Again, in John 18:37, replying to Pilate, Jesus says, 'Everyone who is of the truth hears My voice.' God wants us to hear Him speak to us. He doesn't make it difficult, but we have to want to hear, and be prepared to be obedient.

So how does God speak to us? The easiest thing to recognise is what is often termed 'an inner witness of the Spirit'. This is a feeling that something is either right or wrong. We may say that we do not have peace about a certain course of action. This is the Holy Spirit warning us that it is not the right path to take. A useful piece of scriptural guidance here is in Colossians 3:15, which says, 'let the peace of God rule in your hearts....' The Holy Spirit can speak

51

through the conscience, making us feel uncomfortable about doing anything that is contrary to God's word. We must, however, be careful to ensure that we do not quench this voice of conscience, or we will soon stop hearing it. Sometimes, we may feel quite certain that it is right to do something, even though we neither understand it nor, at another level, really want to do it. This, too, can be inner witness of the Spirit.

Then there are the occasions when, for no apparent reason, a verse of Scripture comes to mind; or perhaps we are reading the Bible when suddenly a verse stands out and becomes alive to us. This is a way in which the Lord makes known one of His *rhema* words to us that we discussed earlier—His word spoken specifically to the individual. If you need to make a decision, it is good to ask God to give you a word like this. Some years ago, I was asked to go with a team of people to do some Bible teaching in Bahrain. The woman who asked me is a dynamic character and an accomplished speaker. Naturally, I felt somewhat inadequate. What could I add to the team? Also, I was not too certain about a woman teaching the Bible in a place where cultural attitudes toward women are quite different from those in the West—and I had seen the way men in some countries look at women! I asked God for a word, to show me whether I should go. Unusually (for me), He gave me a reference. It just came to mind and I looked it up — Jeremiah 1:7–9, 'But the LORD said to me: "Do not say, 'I am a youth.' For you shall go to all to whom I send you, And whatever I command you, you shall speak. Do not be afraid of their faces, For I am with you to deliver you," says the LORD. Then the Lord put forth His hand and touched my mouth, and the LORD said to me: "Behold, I have put My words in your mouth."' Isn't it amazing how specific the word of God is! He dealt precisely with the two things that concerned me, namely my inadequacy to speak and the fear of their faces. God is always willing to confirm His word to us. Two other people had words for me, confirming that it was right for me to go. It is important, though, that we do not act merely on words given by other people; our heavenly Father will speak to us first and then use others to confirm what He has told us. Hearing God in this way is not a matter of 'chance', and it is a dangerous thing to do to open the

Bible at random to find guidance!

At the end of a talk in which I had recalled this incident, a young woman came up to me and said that when I had quoted the verse, '"Do not be afraid of their faces, For I am with you to deliver you," says the LORD', it was as though I had been speaking directly to her, and that it was the only thing I said. She was waiting to testify at a trial against a paedophile ring that had abused her, and was very much afraid of having to recall their faces. The word had been *rhema* to her. She says, 'At the time, I could only see some of the faces within the paedophile ring. These were the names I had given to the police, but there were other faces I couldn't see. The faces had no features at all. I knew I didn't want to see these other faces; I didn't want to admit to myself or the police who they were. As you quoted that verse I felt God saying, "It's OK. I'll help you look at those faces. I will be there with you and hold you; and I will deliver you from all this evil." When you and Don prayed with me, I knew I had to spend time alone with God, allowing the faces to be revealed to me. It was very hard but God kept His promises to me (as He always does!) He held me as I looked, and He is delivering me from all the evil which was done to me. I have been able to give more names to the police since then, as they were made clear to me, as I allowed myself to look at their faces. I can, at times, even pray for some of them now.'

Sometimes, God speaks to us with an inner voice. This can be rather like a persistent thought. Usually, the first thought that comes is from God, and it is often followed by another thought along the lines: 'that's just you thinking it; do that and you will look stupid!' You may wonder whether the thought is your own wishful thinking or God's voice. I have found it helpful to pray that, if it is not of Him, He will take the thought away but, if it is Him speaking, He will constantly bring it to mind. Here, we are speaking of an inner rather than audible voice. Isaiah 30:21 tells us, 'Your ears shall hear a word behind you, saying, "This is the way, walk in it," Whenever you turn to the right hand, or whenever you turn to the left.' Philip heard this voice of the Spirit, when he was told to go and speak to the Ethiopian eunuch in the chariot (Acts 8:29,30). I think particularly of an occasion when God spoke to me very clearly.

The impression was so strong that, although it seemed very unlikely in the natural sense, I was absolutely certain that my husband, Don, was going to get a job in Wiltshire. God said to me that Don would be going back to Trowbridge. At that time there was not even a job being advertised there! Moreover, it seemed most unlikely that he would go back to where he had worked before. Yet, within two weeks a job had been advertised, and two other people had confirmed that God had told them Don should apply for it. As it happened, certain problems arose in the job, which meant that it was really important that Don knew that he was in the right place, and that God had called him to sort them out.

Again, it is important to recognise that the voice is the voice of God. If you have been involved in other religions, some alternative medicines with occult origins, or based in other religions, or with occult practices such as ouija, tarot etc., any voices in the head may be of occult origin, such as spirit guides. In such cases, it is very important to receive ministry for deliverance.

Visions, pictures and dreams are other ways in which God may speak to us. An angel appeared to Joseph in a dream, to warn him to flee to Egypt with the baby Jesus, because King Herod wanted to kill him (Matthew 2:13-14). Paul received a vision of a man from Macedonia, saying, 'Come over to Macedonia and help us.' (Acts 16:9-10). Sometimes, though not always, when we get a very clear word like that, it is because there are going to be difficulties and we need to be absolutely sure that God sent us. We are going to have to stand on the word. Paul and Silas were used powerfully in Philippi, but were also imprisoned there. Once, when I was worshipping the Lord, I got a picture in my mind of the Golden Buddha in Bangkok. At the same time, I heard an inner voice saying, 'My glory I will not give to another.' I was horrified because, although I had been to Bangkok and had entered the Temple of the Golden Buddha, I was sure I had never given glory to it. God then showed me that taking one's shoes off, as I had done, was a mark of respect and an act of worship. I repented immediately, and vowed never to enter a temple to a foreign god again. At the time when I was going to Bahrain, God had promised that He would give me His words to speak. He did this in a quite remarkable way. Night after night before I went, I dreamed that I was standing in front of a crowd of people preaching. When I woke up, I remembered the talks so clearly that I simply wrote them out. I received seven talks in this way. When we arrived in Bahrain and were given our speaking schedules, I discovered that I was required to give seven talks! I just had to ask God which one to deliver in each place.

Occasionally, God speaks in an audible voice. Samuel heard God in this way when he was a child in the Temple. (1 Samuel 3:4–14). Peter, James and John heard God speak audibly on the Mount of Transfiguration, and an audible voice was heard when John baptised Jesus in the Jordan. Saul heard the audible voice of Jesus, on the way to Damascus. (Acts 9:4–6). I have not heard God in this way... yet! But maybe you have.

There are many stories of angels visiting people these days. There was another time when Don was going for an interview for a new job, but was in two minds as to whether it was right for him. As he drove towards Birmingham, he stopped at traffic lights. A tramp leaned into the car, asking for a lift. Don refused. The lights changed and he drove away. Turning round, Don could see no sign of the tramp; he had just vanished. Later, after having pulled out of the second round of interviews, still in turmoil, we discovered that friends had prayed that God would send an angel to direct him. And Don had refused to give him a lift! I am reminded of Hebrews 13:2. 'Do not forget to entertain strangers, for by so doing some have unwittingly entertained angels.' Please note, I am not advocating that you should always pick up hitchhikers! Prudence is commended in Scripture. (See Proverbs 8:5). There are numerous occasions cited in the Bible when God has sent angels. An angel was sent to tell Mary that she was to bear Jesus (Luke 1:26–38), and an angel appeared to Zacharias to tell him that his wife, Elizabeth, was to have a son, and his name would be John. (Luke 1:5–25) Often, God sends angels to His servants. Discernment is necessary here, as at every point in the Christian life. In 2 Corinthians 11:14, at the point where Paul is reminding Christians of the existence of false ministries, we read that, 'Satan himself transforms himself into an angel of light.'

A further way in which God speaks is through prophetic ministry. Hebrews 1:1–2 says, 'God, who at various times and in various ways spoke in time past to the fathers by the prophets, has in these last days spoken to us by His Son....' The role of the prophet was extremely important, in that he spoke God's word to the people. Probably the most well known prophet is Jonah, who was sent to warn the city of Nineveh of impending disaster if they did not repent. God still speaks to nations by the mouths of those to whom He has given a prophetic ministry today. In addition to this, God may use people to give prophecies to individuals on specific occasions. Such personal prophecy must always be tested in the light of Scripture, and should confirm something you yourself feel. There was a time when Don was considering a job in London, but did not have any peace about it. Someone, whom we only knew slightly, and who had never been to our house before, called on us and, in the course of conversation, made it clear that he should not take the job. Immediately, we both felt a sense of relief. Of course, as the verse in Hebrews suggests, the Bible is the main way in which we get guidance. Again, discernment must be exercised — a word from someone with a prophetic gift or ministry may contain something of the Lord and something of the flesh, even something of the person's own commonsense! Much depends upon the faithfulness of the one delivering the word. (For a discussion of this topic, see *Growing in the Prophetic* by Mike Bickle, Kingsway 1995.) There are biblical criteria to be used in evaluating a prophetic word. It is a ministry to be desired by Christians (1 Corinthians 14:1), some are called to it (Ephesians 4:11), yet those ministering in this gift are not to be regarded as infallible (1 Corinthians 14:32), and we are to beware of the danger of falsehood in this area of ministry (2 Peter 2:1 and 1 John 4:1).

You will sometimes hear Christians speak of using 'fleeces'. This refers to the incident recorded in Judges 6:36–40, in which Gideon sought guidance from God by placing a fleece on the floor and asking for its wetness or dryness the next day to be an indicator of the Lord's will. This is not to be recommended these days. In Gideon's day, the Holy Spirit had not been given, except to specific people or for specific tasks. Asking for guidance by requiring God to fulfil a specific set of circumstances is a risky business, as Satan can fulfil them too. It is not a reliable way to get guidance, as some people have found to their cost. God has some harsh things to say about those who require signs. Jesus said, 'An evil and adulterous generation seeks after a sign' (Matthew12:39). God has given us His word and His Spirit to guide us, and He expects us to walk by faith.

In conclusion, God wants us to hear His voice and does not make it difficult for us. It is just a matter of learning to recognise when He is speaking to us, in the same way as we learn to recognise anyone's voice. He will teach us as long as we are willing. Probably the first things He asks us to do or speak will not be too disastrous if we get it wrong. It is advisable to say, 'I think God is saying this', rather than 'Thus says the Lord!' Then, if someone acknowledges that it applies to him or her, we will know that it was indeed God's voice that we heard. Many years ago, when I was trying to learn how to recognise God's voice, I felt Him tell me to visit a particular person. On the way, I passed the house of another friend and decided to visit her instead! She was out, so I went on to the person I was meant to see, who said, 'I was praying for someone to come.'

What is absolutely essential is that everything we do or say must be in accordance with God's word, the Bible. This has to be the ultimate test. **Anything that we think God has said to us but which disagrees with Scripture cannot be God speaking to us, because God does not contradict His word.**

Chapter Thirteen

THE NEW COVENANT

For He made Him who knew no sin to be sin for us,
that we might become the righteousness of God in Him.

2 Corinthians 5:21

Under the old covenant, Abraham was promised land, descendants (the Jewish people), and blessings, which have resulted in that people's success as a nation: success in business and their survival — despite many attempts to eradicate them; and blessing for all nations of the earth, because of the 'coming seed' Jesus, the redeemer. The old covenant is the foundation for the new covenant. 'For the law, having a shadow of the good things to come, and not the very image of the things....' (Hebrews 10:1). In Galatians 4:22–26,31, we read how Abraham's two sons, Ishmael and Isaac, are symbolic of the two covenants. Hagar was a servant, and produced Ishmael, born according to the flesh, whereas Sarah was a free woman, and produced Isaac, as a result of the promise. Thus, the old covenant represented bondage to law, and justification was by obedience to the law; but the new covenant represents freedom, and justification is by faith.

God knew that the Israelites would not be able to keep the conditions of the law, so He had instituted the sacrifices to cover (atone) for their sin. However, as we have seen, this was only a temporary solution, as sacrifices of animals could never take away the sins (Hebrews 10:4), so, through the prophets Jeremiah and Ezekiel, He spoke of a time when He was going to make a new covenant with His people.

Under the terms of the old covenant, on the Day of Atonement the high priest first made a sacrifice for his own sins, then entered the Holy of Holies, with the blood to put on the mercy seat

58

for the sins of the people. (See Hebrews 9:1–8.) Jesus, as mediator of the new covenant, being sinless, did not have to make a sacrifice for his own sin, but was a perfect High Priest—not after the order of Levi, but after the order of Melchizedek, the high priest in the heavenly Jerusalem, who had come, not with a sacrificial lamb, but with bread and wine, symbolising the body and blood of Jesus. Melchizedek was both priest and king. Jesus was supremely Priest and King. The Levitical priests could never be kings, and someone from the tribe of Judah could not become a priest, but Jesus is the King of righteousness and King of Salem (peace), as well as being the High Priest of our confession. (See Hebrews 7:24–28).

Whereas the old covenant demanded regular sacrifices for sin, Jesus' perfect sacrifice was once and for all. (See Hebrews 9:11–12.) There was no further need for sacrifice, as he had not simply atoned for sins, but had totally remitted them. He had presented his own blood in the temple, in the heavenly Jerusalem (Hebrews 4:14). This is the reason why Jesus told Mary not to touch him, after he was resurrected (John 20:17). He had not yet ascended and presented his blood in heaven. On the cross, when Jesus cried out, 'It is finished', he was showing that he had completed the old covenant (See Hebrews 9:15; Romans 8:3).

Under the old covenant, the priest carried incense from the golden altar of incense, through the veil, into the Holy of Holies once a year on the Day of Atonement (Leviticus 16:11–13), but the writer to the Hebrews puts the altar of incense inside the Holy of Holies. (See Hebrews 9:1–5.) In other words, we live in the Day of Atonement. When Jesus took our sin on the cross, the veil of the temple, separating the Holy of Holies from the Holy Place was torn in two from top to bottom (Luke 23:45), signifying that the way was now open for us to approach the mercy seat of God (Hebrews 10:19,20). [See Appendix, page 94, for a plan of the Tabernacle.]

When Jesus became surety of the new covenant, he made it possible for the Gentiles, as well as the Jews, to enter into that covenant relationship with himself. On the Temple Mount, the court of the Gentiles was separated from the Temple itself by the 'wall of partition.' Ephesians 2:14 refers to the fact that Jesus has broken down the middle wall of partition between the Jews and the Gentiles. Belonging to Jesus Christ makes us Gentiles Abraham's seed too.

As partakers of the new covenant we have an exchange of identities with Jesus: he takes our sin nature, and we take his righteousness. I like to think of this as 'the royal exchange'! There is an end to living separately from Christ (Galatians 2:20). Since Jesus took on himself the curses of the Law, sickness, poverty and spiritual death (Isaiah 53:4,5; 2 Corinthians 8:9), we no longer have to suffer the consequences of the broken covenant. Instead, we can have the blessings, which were physical, spiritual and material, (1 Peter 2:24; Ephesians 1:3; Philippians 4:19). Above all, we are given the promised Holy Spirit. The Lord's Supper becomes the covenant meal, the bread representing not only the paschal lamb, but also Jesus' own body; the cup representing not only the shed blood of the paschal lamb, but his own blood. This is the cup of redemption or the cup of blessing.

Finally, as part of our covenant exchanges, we have the right to use the name of Jesus. This is the most wonderful covenant privilege. There is great power in the precious name of Jesus for all believers, born again of the Spirit of God. Our standing in the new covenant, as adopted children, means that when we pray and when we exercise our delegated authority according to the Scriptures, we can ask our Father with all the confidence of children of the covenant. He is committed to giving His children good things. He will keep His side of the covenant and will honour His promises to us!

Chapter Fourteen

THE LAW OF SOWING AND REAPING

Do not be deceived, God is not mocked; for
whatever a man sows, that he will also reap.
Galatians 6:7

There is a story told about a skunk. The wind changed and it all came back to him! This illustrates very well the law of sowing and reaping. God's principle is that what you sow is what you reap. Paul says, 'Do not be deceived, God is not mocked; for whatever a man sows, that he will also reap' (Galatians 6:7). There is a proverb which says, 'Whoever digs a pit will fall into it, and he who rolls a stone will have it roll back on him' (Proverbs 26:27). Jesus says, 'And just as you want men to do to you, you also do to them likewise' (Luke 6:31). God Himself provides the right pattern for positive sowing and reaping: He loved us first; we are to respond in love to His love, which He has shown towards us in Jesus.

This principle of sowing and reaping applies in the natural world. 'Then God said, "Let the earth bring forth grass, the herb that yields seed, and the fruit tree that yields fruit according to its kind..."' (Genesis 1:11). We can see that, whatever kind of seed was sown, the fruit it produced was of the same type.

Jesus teaches us, 'Judge not, and you shall not be judged. Condemn not, and you shall not be condemned' (Luke 6:37). It is so important not to be judgmental and critical. It is very easy to become negative, and to allow a critical spirit to establish a place in our lives, but people who become like this are neither happy themselves nor do they bring blessing to others. We must try always to be positive and to give words of encouragement. This is particularly important in bringing up children, but also important if you are an employer and want to get the best out of your staff. Encouragers are a pleasure to be with, and a pleasure to work for. If we want to be encouraged, we must sow encouragement.

Sowing and reaping applies in the area of mercy and forgiveness. Justice without mercy can simply produce rebellion. James tells us that mercy triumphs over judgement. We can only be forgiven if we, ourselves, forgive others (see Mark 11:26). In the Lord's prayer, Jesus teaches us that it is in the measure that we forgive others that we ourselves can be forgiven. 'For if you forgive men their trespasses, your heavenly Father will also forgive you. But if you do not forgive men their trespasses, neither will your Father forgive your trespasses' (Matthew 6:14,15). The parable of the unforgiving servant shows us how the Father responds to those who refuse to forgive (see Matthew 18:21-35).

In the area of giving, we reap according to the measure by which we have given. (See Luke 6:38.) Paul tells us that, 'He who sows sparingly will also reap sparingly, and he who sows bountifully will also reap bountifully' (2 Corinthians 9:6). There has been much misunderstanding concerning this teaching on giving, often with disastrous consequences. It is not a 'get rich quick' formula. We do not give in order to get back. Rather, we give as God directs, and in obedience to Him. Nevertheless, God loves to bless us, because that is His nature. We give because we love Him. Paul tells us that God loves a joyful giver. He then goes on to say, 'And God is able to make all grace abound toward you, that you, always having all sufficiency in all things, may have an abundance for every good work' (9:8). This is the best definition of prosperity. It means 'having enough to meet all our own needs, and sufficient to bless others.' Paul continues praying, 'Now may He who supplies seed to the sower, and bread for food, supply and multiply the seed you have sown and increase the fruits of your righteousness.' (2 Corinthians 9:10). We see here that as we give to Him, He will ensure that we have 'bread for food' and 'more seed to give away'. This is God's principle of seed faith.

Some years ago we gave money to a family to enable them to go to America for their son's wedding. We had no thought of getting anything in return. However, many years later, God prompted another Christian friend to give us a holiday at a time when we were in need of a rest. This is how God's economy works. God will trust with riches only those people that He knows will be completely obedient, using it in the way He tells them. Many Christian businessmen are used to support full-time evangelists. God blesses their businesses, and they use their money to support His work.

God makes another promise to those who tithe. Malachi 3:10,11 says, "Bring all the tithes into the storehouse, that there may be food in My house. And try Me now in this," says the LORD of hosts, "If I will not open for you the windows of heaven And pour out for you such blessing That there will not be room enough to receive it. And I will rebuke the devourer for your sakes, So that he will not destroy the fruit of your ground...." A farmer we know was having trouble with crows eating his wheat, so he reminded the Lord that He had promised to rebuke the devourer on his behalf. He then told the crows to go. The next morning there were none to be seen.

God wills that we should sow so readily and generously that we will reap abundant blessings ourselves. Sadly, people sometimes sow negative things, like bitterness. If we allow bitterness into our hearts, sowing it in our thoughts and words, we will reap destruction. Bitterness is often (but not always) the root cause of arthritis. We saw a lady forget to take her walking stick with her in her excitement at being healed when she had spoken out forgiveness for her husband who had mistreated her. The Bible teaches us that the way to overcome evil is with good. God commands us to bless those who hurt us or treat us unfairly, neither dwelling on the wrong nor harbouring bitter thoughts. It may seem hard, but we can choose to obey God in this area, by an act of our will. It always works! 'See that no one renders evil for evil to anyone, but always pursue what is good both for yourselves and for all' (1 Thessalonians 5:15). And we read in 1 Peter 3:9, '...not returning evil for evil or reviling for reviling, but on the contrary blessing, knowing that you were called to this, that you may inherit a blessing.' Someone who had been particularly difficult at my husband's workplace changed noticeably after we had spent time praying for him and his family to be blessed. In fact, someone else remarked, 'Whatever has happened to him? He is so different these days.' After receiving prayer for healing, a member of our house group received both considerable relief in physical symptoms and a wider healing of broken relationships within the family. Reconciliation occurred between him, and his father and stepmother, after twelve years of estrangement. This was followed by a reunion between his father, stepmother, sister and her family, after twenty three years without contact. The tears of his nephew, now a young man, on hearing the news that he was at last to see his grandfather, was just one of the sources of joy in the process of healing. However, there was a slight 'blip' which occurred when his stepmother failed to contact him when his father became ill and was taken into hospital. Naturally hurt, he immediately put into practice the principle of praying blessings on her. Soon after, they were able to spend part of Christmas together as a family for the first time in many years. Let us learn to live by Galatians 6:10, 'Therefore, as we have opportunity, let us do good to all, especially to those who are of the household of faith.'

Finally, it is probably worth noting that the Bible tells us that 'in due season we shall reap...' (Galatians 6:9). There is often a waiting time between the sowing and the reaping.

Chapter Fifteen

MEDITATING THE WORD

This Book of the Law shall not depart from your mouth, but you shall meditate in it day and night, that you may observe to do according to all that is written in it. For then you will make your way prosperous, and then you will have good success.

Joshua 1:8

We have seen that, in order to grow in Christian maturity, we need to know and obey the written word of God, and that we must allow His words to become His *rhema* words to us personally. The word of God begins to shape our thinking, our actions, our responses, as it becomes part of us. It is crucial that our thinking must be renewed in accordance with the word of God. In Colossians 3:2, Paul encourages us to set our minds 'on things above, not on things on the earth.' In his letter to the Philippians (4:8), he gives us a list of suitable things to meditate on.

Repeatedly, the psalmist declares that he meditates on God's word day and night. To 'meditate' means to ponder, turn over in the mind, imagine, mutter, speak. It involves active recitation; it is not merely a mental exercise. Not only can we think about the subject, but also allow our imagination to become involved, and then speak, mutter or murmur it to ourselves. Often, David encouraged himself by speaking to his soul! This allows it to go from the mind into the spirit, where it will produce fruit. What we meditate determines the kind of fruit that is produced (see Luke 6:45). James describes the two kinds of fruits in James 3:12–18.

Yoga meditation, and transcendental meditation, are designed to make the mind blank. Their purpose is to induce a state of trance, supposedly allowing the mind to be drawn upwards to become yoked with hindu deity. 'All forms of yoga suspend the reasoning powers

65

and enable spirits to possess it.' (Johanna Michaelsen, former yoga teacher, author of *The Beautiful Side of Evil*). It is possible for evil spirits to fill the emptied mind with thoughts which are often frightening or destructive. Fantasy games of violence and witchcraft often lead to obsession which, on occasion, has resulted in terrible acts of torture, or even murder. Such was the case with the perpetrator of the Hungerford massacre. Similarly, studies have revealed that those who spend time looking at pornographic literature and videos become hardened in their attitudes, and may graduate to rape and sexual abuse. Watching horror movies can allow fear to control us. At a less extreme level, we can meditate on our mistakes and failures, constantly reliving them. Doing this will lead to depression and fear. In contrast, if we choose to meditate instead on good things, our spirits are lifted. Praising God not only delights Him but can make us feel better too!

We have a choice concerning what we meditate. When we meditate the Scriptures, we are filling our minds with the word of God. This establishes the word in our hearts, because the mind is the gateway to the spirit. As we meditate on the goodness of God, (in Psalm 103:1–19, for example), our faith is built up. Our love for God increases. Meditating on Psalm 91 helps us to overcome fear. Psalm 112:1,7–8 teaches that the person who delights in God's commandments will not be afraid because his heart is established, trusting in the Lord. He will not be shaken when bad news comes. Meditating healing Scriptures increases our faith to receive healing. Meditating verses about God's love, such as Romans 8:31–39, will deal with rejection and low-self worth. Meditating on the covenant names of God helps us to praise Him. Meditating on the titles given to Jesus will fill us with love and praise for him. In Philippians 4:8, Paul encourages us to meditate on things that are pure, praiseworthy and lovely. David was called a man after God's own heart, and he constantly meditated on God's word. In Psalm 4:4, he says, 'Meditate within your heart on your bed, and be still.' And in Psalm 19:14, there is the plea that the meditations of his heart will please the Lord. Other psalms refer to meditating day and night, (and God can speak into your spirit when you are asleep, if you meditate on Him last thing at night); meditating on the works of His hands, contemplating all God's ways; and meditating His laws. They describe how meditation on God's laws brings blessing and prosperity (See Psalm 1). Wisdom, understanding and discernment come from meditating on God's word; so does peace of mind. We are encouraged not merely to read the Scriptures, but to study them and to meditate on them — if we desire to grow and bear good fruit. (John 15:7–8).

Chapter Sixteen

LOVE, ACCEPTANCE & FORGIVENESS

For I am persuaded that neither death nor life, nor
angels nor principalities nor powers, nor things present
nor things to come, nor height nor depth, nor any other
created thing, shall be able to separate us from the
love of God which is in Christ Jesus our Lord.

Romans 8:38,39

Maturity is expressing God's love. Faith and hope are not worth anything without love, because faith works through love. Whenever we read about Jesus healing anyone, we remember that he had compassion upon the sick. Love focuses the power of God. In James 2:8, Jesus' instruction, 'You shall love your neighbour as yourself' is described as the 'royal law'.

In Greek, there are four words used to describe four different kinds of love. *Philia* is friendship; the kind of tender affection based on what we like about a person. It does not overlook faults, and can quickly turn to hate when wronged. It may even become a controlling love. *Storge* is brotherly love; the affection one has for one's family. *Eros* describes sexual attraction, which leads to lust rather than true love. The God kind of love is *agape*. It is an unselfish and unconditional love, which requires nothing in return. Since it is based on an act of will rather than emotion, it does not depend on the nature of the person who is loved. Jesus' is *agape* love. The word *agape* is not found in classical Greek before the time of Jesus.

Jesus requires us to love him with *agape* love. When Jesus asked Peter at breakfast by the Sea of Galilee if he loved him (John 21:15–17), Jesus used the verb *agape*, but Peter answered that he loved him using the verb *phileo*. This happened a second time, then Jesus asked the question a third time, now using a form of *phileo*. If we love God for what He has done for us, it is *philia* love; if we love Him for who He is, it is *agape*.

God's love for us is *agape* love; it does not depend on our loving Him in return. 'We love Him because He first loved us' (1 John 4:19). Nor does it depend on our deserving such love. Romans 5:8 shows us the nature of God's love for us, '...in that while we were still sinners, Christ died for us.' It is comforting to know that nothing 'shall be able to separate us from the love of God which is in Christ Jesus our Lord' (Romans 8:38,39). As God said to Jeremiah, 'I have loved you with an everlasting love.' If we really know how much God loves us, we have total security. Paul describes the love of Christ as that which 'passes knowledge'. He desires that 'you may... be strong to apprehend and grasp with all the saints (God's devoted people, the experience of that love) what is the breadth and length and height and depth (of it); That you may really come to know — practically, through experience for yourselves — the love of Christ, which far surpasses mere knowledge (without experience)' (Ephesians 3:18,19) [AMP]. When we understand the depths of God's love, there is no room for fear. His 'perfect love casts out fear' (1 John 4:18).

How is *agape* love demonstrated? It seeks the welfare of others (Romans 15:2). It doesn't work ill to anyone (see Romans 13:8ff). *Agape* love seeks opportunities to do good (Galatians 6:10). *Agape* love is compassionate (Romans 12:15). *Agape* love always forgives (Colossians 3:13,14); serves others (1 Corinthians 9:19); puts others first (Philippians 2:2,3); makes allowances for others (Ephesians 4:2). Paul gives a comprehensive description of *agape* love in 1 Cor 13:4–7. It may be helpful to test ourselves by replacing the word love with our own name, e.g. the love of God in ..... is patient, is kind. The love of God in ..... doesn't envy or boil over with jealousy ..... doesn't boast and isn't arrogant ..... isn't rude and never insists on *his/her* own way. .....is not selfish. ..... isn't touchy or fretful and doesn't let *his/her* feelings get hurt. ..... takes no account of the evil done to *him/her* and does not hold grudges. ..... believes the best in every person and never loses hope.

Jesus said that the whole of the law is summed up in the commandment, 'You shall love your neighbour as yourself' (Galatians

5:14). John teaches us that the test of whether we know God is whether we keep His commandments, and the commandment of God is that we should love as He loves. 'He who says he abides in Him ought himself also to walk just as He walked' (1 John 2:6); and, 'as He is, so are we in this world' (1 John 4:17). Jesus came to reveal the Father's nature to the world in *agape* love. This is also what we must be to the world. Paul teaches us that we should put on love above all things. (See Colossians 3:14) Just as faith causes man to *act* like God, love causes man to *be* like God. Paul tells us that he is 'compelled' by the love of God. (See 2 Corinthians 5:14). To walk in love is to be our greatest aim in life. Paul's prayer for the Thessalonians was that the Lord would make them 'increase and abound in love to one another and to all', just as he did to them (see 1 Thessalonians 3:12).

Does this all sound too difficult to achieve? This kind of love is not the result of our emotions, but is an act of will: we can choose to love like Jesus. The Holy Spirit then makes it possible. (See Romans 5:5; Galatians 5:22). I have found that, if I am finding someone difficult to love, but ask God to give me love for that person, He will. God does not change them, but He will change how I feel about them.

Love says, 'You are accepted.' As we know that we have been adopted into the family of God, and so are His children, then we know that we are totally accepted. We read in Ephesians 1:5,6, '...having predestined us to adoption as sons by Jesus Christ to Himself, according to the good pleasure of His will, to the praise of the glory of His grace, by which He has made us accepted in the Beloved.' To know in this way that we are acceptable is true security.

The supreme way in which love manifests itself is in forgiveness. *Agape* love always forgives. God is always willing to forgive when we repent. 'If we confess our sins, He is faithful and just to forgive us our sins and to cleanse us from all unrighteousness' (1 John 1:9). Jesus demonstrated his heart of forgiveness when he said from the cross, 'Father forgive them, for they do not know what they do.' Jesus often taught about the importance of forgiveness. He explained that, if we do not forgive, then our Heavenly Father cannot forgive us. (See Matt 6:14,15; Mark 11:26). This is borne out by Jesus' teaching on prayer. He taught his disciples to pray: 'Forgive us our sins, for we also forgive everyone who is indebted to us.' He also explained that, if we have unforgiveness in our hearts, we cannot expect to receive anything from God. Moreover, in the parable of the unforgiving servant, Jesus shows that unforgiveness leads to mental torment. (Matthew 18:21–35). He tells Peter that he must continue to forgive, and not keep account of wrongs, saying that he should forgive 'up to seventy times seven.' If we are to be like Jesus, and become the kind of obedient Christians God wants us to be, we must learn to forgive, and be constantly, continually forgiving. Whenever we fail in this area, we need to repent immediately, get right with God again, and change our attitude toward any who seem to us to have offended.

Chapter Seventeen

EFFECTIVE PRAYER

*'Whatever things you ask when you pray, believe
that you receive them, and you will have them.'*
Mark 11:24

James 5:16 states, ' The effective, fervent prayer of a righteous man
avails much.' Or, as the amplified version says, 'The earnest (heart-
felt, continued) prayer of a righteous man makes tremendous power
available — dynamic in its working.'[AMP]. Frank Laubach described prayer as the mightiest force in the world, and Kenneth
Copeland said, 'prayer is the doorway into the mightiest release of
power known to man.' James makes it clear that we do not have to
be someone special to get our prayers answered as he says that Elijah
was just like us. (James 5:17–18). It seems the important thing is to
pray earnestly. You may ask, 'why do I need to pray, when God
already knows our needs?' The answer is that God wills that we
should. James 4:2 says, 'You do not have because you do not ask.'
Jesus says, 'Ask, and it will be given to you; seek, and you will
find; knock, and it will be opened to you' (Matthew 7:7). Amaz-
ingly, Charles Wesley states, 'It seems that God is limited by our
prayer life and that He can do nothing for humanity unless someone
asks Him.' Although God is omnipotent, yet He has chosen to work
through our prayers; He wants us to work together with Him. God
will not usually intervene unless we ask. He is unwilling to override
our will. With this responsibility, and the tremendous power available to us, it is obviously important that we understand the principles of prayer and the reasons for unanswered prayer.

Firstly, Jesus teaches us to pray to the Father (Luke11:2). He
explained to the disciples that the time was coming when he would
return to the Father and he says that then they will not ask him but

will ask the Father (John 16:23ff). 'In that day you will ask in My name, and I do not say to you that I shall pray the Father for you; for the Father Himself loves you, because you have loved Me, and have believed that I came forth from God' (John 16:26). So we should ask the Father in the name of Jesus. Jesus said, 'I chose you and appointed you that you should go and bear fruit, and that your fruit should remain, that whatever you ask the Father in My name He may give you' (John 15:16). We should note that there is a condition—that we should bear lasting fruit. 'When you pray, go into your room, and when you have shut your door, pray to your Father who is in the secret place' (Matthew 6:6). Here, Jesus is not, of course, saying we can only pray in our bedrooms, but he is saying that we should not make a public show of our prayers to appear 'holy', as the Pharisees did.

Prayer should not be a 'hit or miss' affair. We should be able to pray with the confident expectation that we shall receive the desired answer. There are, however, certain principles that apply. We have seen from Mark 11:24 that **believing is a requirement for receiving**. It is the prayer of faith that gets the answer. We read in James 5:15, 'And the prayer of faith will save the sick, and the Lord will raise him up. And if he has committed sins, he will be forgiven.' It is the *faith* expressed in the prayer that gets him healed. We receive our healing by faith in the work of Jesus on the cross and, in the same way, by grace through faith our sins are forgiven. Recently, we were asked to pray for someone who had just been diagnosed as having a tumour. It had shown up on the scan and was two and a half centimetres in diameter. She had faith to believe that, if we prayed, God would cause the tumour to disappear. When she went into hospital a few days later, the surgeon removed a few cells and sent them off for analysis. The answer came back that it was 'inconclusive'! She was called back two weeks later for another appointment, and the surgeon removed something more. While she waited for the results, she asked God to give her a sign to show her what had happened. She felt sure the tumour was gradually shrinking in response to our prayer. The next day, two hot air balloons came over the house. One landed in a nearby field. As she watched, the balloon deflated and began to shrink. She knew that was her sign. The results came back, indicating that the tumour was now very small and superficial. Jesus said to the father of a child suffering from convulsions caused by a 'mute spirit', 'If you can believe, all things are possible to him who believes' (Mark 9:23). This is not to bring us into condemnation; we all find it difficult to believe sometimes. However, the Bible clearly teaches that unless we believe we will not receive answers to our prayers. So we need to meditate on the word, and hear the word, until we do have faith for the answer. Jesus also explained the importance of the prayer of agreement. 'Again I say to you that if two of you agree on earth concerning anything that they ask, it will be done for them by My Father in heaven' (Matthew 18:19). Prayer made in this way is very powerful.

Another requirement is that we are to be specific. Vague prayers get vague answers! God says 'ask', not 'hint'. Jesus said, 'If you abide in Me and My words abide in you, you will ask what you desire, and it shall be done for you' (John 15:7). Jesus encourages you to ask for what you desire. Spell it out! Many years ago, when I was looking for a teaching job, I had very specific requirements. I could only work part-time and I wanted to teach 'A' level only. When Jesus says, 'And whatever you ask in My name, that I will do, that the Father may be glorified in the Son' (John 14:13), the meaning of the Greek is 'if I don't have it, I will make it for you.' This is exactly what he did for me. Through meeting someone at a coffee party, I heard that the Headmaster of a local Christian school was looking for someone to teach 'A' level biology part-time…. and it was a new post! It is very unusual to have a teaching job which requires only 'A' level teaching. Again, there is a condition which we must fulfil. It is that we abide in Him and His words abide in us. We must put God first in our lives and be filled with His word. Psalm 37:4,5 says, 'Delight yourself also in the LORD, and He shall give you the desires of your heart. Commit your way to the LORD, Trust also in Him, And He shall bring it to pass.'

If we are to pray with confidence, we must pray according to God's will. 'Now this is the confidence that we have in Him, that if we ask anything according to His will, He hears us. And if we know that He hears us, whatever we ask, we know that we have the peti-

74

tions that we have asked of Him (1 John 5:14,15). Paul, in his letter to the Ephesians, says, 'Therefore do not be unwise, but understand what the will of the Lord is' (5:17). We learn what God's will is as we study His word. Therefore, true prayer is word-based prayer. God is moved every time we declare His word and His will in our circumstances. **Effective prayer means taking into God's presence His own words.**

We must, then, ask boldly—expecting that God will do it. Hebrews 4:16 says, 'Let us therefore come boldly to the throne of grace, that we may obtain mercy and find grace to help in time of need.' And Hebrews 10:19 assures us that we can have boldness to come to the Holiest, because of the blood which Jesus shed for us on the cross.

As we have seen, for prayer to be answered, there are conditions which must be fulfilled. There are certain things which will hinder our prayers. James makes it clear that we cannot get our prayers answered if we entertain doubt. He teaches that a person who doubts is not to suppose that he will receive anything from the Lord. (See James 1:6.7).

We have already considered the area of forgiveness, noting that it is essential. Unforgiveness will prevent our getting answers to our prayers. Jesus said, 'whenever you stand praying, if you have anything against anyone, forgive him....' Many people have been healed the moment they have forgiven someone who has hurt them. On one occasion when Don was speaking, a girl had taken her non-Christian boyfriend to the meeting. After much struggling, she finally forgave her father—who had left her and her mother when she was a small child. As soon as she forgave, her boyfriend (for whom she had been praying) gave his life to the Lord.

We cannot expect the Lord to hear our prayer when there is unconfessed sin in our lives. (See Psalm 66:18). God told the people of Israel through Isaiah His prophet, 'I cannot endure iniquity'; and, 'Even though you make many prayers, I will not hear.' This was because their 'hands are full of blood' (from Isaiah 1:13,15). It is only when we do not have sin in our lives that our hearts do not condemn us and we know we shall have what we ask. (See 1 John 3:21,22).

75

As marriage is ordained by God, it is the strongest relationship in the world. As such, the prayer of agreement between marriage partners is an extremely powerful prayer. However, Peter teaches that if the husband does not have a right attitude toward his wife, his prayers will be hindered. (See 1 Peter 3:7.)

Wrong motives, such as selfishness or pride, will also hinder our prayers. James tells the Israelites, 'You ask and do not receive, because you ask amiss, that you may spend it on your pleasures' (James 4:3). We have to 'call upon the Lord out of a pure heart' (2 Timothy 2:22).

Worship, praise and thankfulness are important ingredients of prayer. 'Now we know that God does not hear sinners; but if anyone is a worshiper of God and does His will, He hears him' (John 9:31). The principle of giving thanks *in* everything is set out in 1 Thessalonians 5:16–18. It is important to understand: it does not say we should give thanks *for* everything, because many of the things that happen are not from God; but we can learn to overcome, if we give thanks to God for all His goodness to us, even though the circumstances at the time may not be good. When God answers our prayers, it is most important that we remember to thank Him.

Worry amounts to lack of trust. We have friends who used to say, 'Why pray when you can worry?' If we are still worrying after we have prayed, it is obvious we do not really believe that God will answer our prayers. Val is a history teacher in a large comprehensive school. Recently, her classroom burnt down and all her textbooks were destroyed, together with her notes and records. Her colleagues could not understand why she was so calm about it, and did not seem to be worrying. But she and her husband had prayed about it and then left it with God to sort out. A few months later, Val's husband was at a Christian businessmen's meeting and had thought that the person giving out the notices sounded like a teacher! He found out that the man was a history teacher and had been teaching the same period as Val, but was now changing to a different syllabus and no longer needed his textbooks. For the cost of the transport, amounting to about £40, Val received thousands of pounds worth of replacement textbooks, far exceeding the number she had originally possessed. God's answers are always 'more than we can ask or think.'

Weariness, half-heartedness, or giving up, may stop us from receiving the answers to our prayers. It is often hard to go on praying and thanking God for something when it doesn't seem to be coming! However, Jesus teaches us to be persistent in prayer. I have heard of people praying for many years for friends or relatives to come to the Lord before it has happened. A friend of ours tells us that someone prayed for her for eight years, and had just said to his wife, 'I don't think I shall pray for her any more' when he received a letter from her, telling him that she had just become a Christian. During the time of persistence, it helps to remind ourselves of God's promises regarding prayer.

There is something about God's timing which we do not always understand. Sometimes it is revealed to us later. A member of our prayer group runs a company which specifies, builds and operates power stations. Proposals which covered all the technical and financial aspects of the work had been submitted to several clients, and he asked for prayer that God's favour would be seen with contracts resulting. There was no progress over a number of weeks, and negotiations all seemed to grind to a halt. It was then discovered that, for various reasons, had any one of the contracts been signed at that time, the company could have been bankrupted. The delay had actually served to avoid that disaster. God's timing is always perfect, which is why we need to have patience and perseverance.

Finally, pride can be a great hindrance to receiving answers to prayer. Micah 6:8 says, 'He has shown you, O man, what is good; and what does the LORD require of you but to do justly, to love mercy, and to walk humbly with your God?' God promises that when the people humble themselves and pray and seek Him and turn from their wickedness, He will hear. (See 2 Chronicles 7:14). The secret of getting our prayers answered is to pray the right thing, in the right way and with the right attitude.

Chapter Eighteen

SPIRITUAL WARFARE

He who is in you is greater than he who is in the world.

1 John 4:4b

This is not the kind of war we volunteer for. We become Satan's enemies the moment we are born again — so we are automatically involved in the battle. It is, therefore, very important that we should be well equipped, knowing how to fight, and who we are fighting. Often we don't see beyond the flesh realm, and try to fight against people, systems or organisations. Scripture teaches that it is not against flesh and blood that we need to fight, but against the spiritual hosts of Satan's army. (See Ephesians 6:12.) 'For though we walk in the flesh, we do not war according to the flesh' (2 Corinthians 10:3).

It is important that we should not underestimate the power of Satan. If we do not understand how he operates, we are likely to be taken in by him. Make no mistake, Satan is in control of this world. We only have to look at many of the terrible things that happen and are recorded in the news each day to realise this. He is referred to in the Bible as 'the ruler of this world' and 'the god of this age' and 'the prince of the power of the air, the spirit that is at work in the sons of disobedience.' However, the Christian is no longer under his control. 'For sin shall not have dominion over you...' (Romans 6:14). We no longer belong to Satan's kingdom; we are not his subjects. 'He [God] has delivered us from the power of darkness and conveyed us into the kingdom of the Son of His love' (Colossians 1:13). Satan is powerful, but not omnipotent. He is variously described as the wicked one, the tempter, the accuser of the brethren, a murderer and the father of lies, Apollyon — the destroyer, Belial —the spirit of worthlessness and emptiness and the devourer. His aim is, and has always been, to separate man from God, and to make him doubt God's goodness and His word. **The battleground is the mind**. This is where he puts his thoughts and tries to make us believe his lies. He tells us things like; 'there is no hope in your situation', 'you are useless', 'you cannot cope', 'you cannot be forgiven', that something bad that is happening is 'God's will', etc. This is why it is vital that we know God's word, so that we are not deceived by such things. Once we learn to recognise his strategy, we will find it much easier to overcome him. Paul tells the Corinthian church that believers have spiritual weapons by which they can cast down arguments that exalt themselves against the knowledge of God, and can bring every thought under the Lordship of Christ. As Satan accuses the brethren, tells us that we are no good, that there is no hope, that 'a Christian does not behave like that', we can come into a false sense of condemnation. This leads to despair, guilt and remorse. But Romans 8:1 assures us that there is no condemnation for those who are in Christ Jesus. When we repent we are forgiven. The Holy Spirit may convict us of wrongdoing — not so that we get into condemnation, but so that we can repent and be restored. We cannot defeat Satan if we are feeling guilty; we must know we are forgiven.

It is important that we do not get ourselves unnecessarily in conflict with demonic powers. It is foolish to challenge Satan unless we are filled with the Holy Spirit, led by the Holy Spirit to do so, and filled with the word of God. We once met someone who had challenged Satan by standing on the altar of a witches' coven, and praying against them. As a result, she had suffered many physical and emotional problems. This is not designed to make anyone afraid, but to make you aware of the danger of acting foolishly, on your own, and when not clearly led by the Spirit to do so.

There are several ways in which we can allow Satan footholds in our lives. Satan cannot act illegally (i.e. against the laws of God in the word of God), which is why he was unable to harm Jesus — because there was no sin in Jesus. (See Luke 4:28–30 and John 14:30). He was not able to take Jesus' life from him; Jesus laid it down. (See John 10:17,18.) We can give Satan squatter's rights by refusing to forgive someone, by getting into pride, or by allowing envy and selfishness to control us. These things will pull down our hedge of protection. (See Ecclesiastes 10:8.) Also, although Satan has no creative power of his own, he can use our own words against us. Things we speak can then become self-fulfilling prophecies.

It is also important not to overestimate Satan's power. Paul writes to the Christians in Rome, 'Yet in all these things [*tribulation, distress, persecution, famine, nakedness, peril or sword*] we are more than conquerors through Him who loved us'(Romans 8:37). Satan has already been defeated completely, and for ever, by Jesus— by his death on the cross and by his resurrection. The only power he has left is the power that people give him. Jesus said to his disciples, 'Behold I give you the authority... over all the power of the enemy, and nothing shall by any means hurt you' (Luke 10:19). John tells us that the power we have in us (the power of the Holy Spirit) is greater than the power that is in the world (the power of Satan).

There are several weapons we have been given, with which to overcome the attacks of the enemy. The name of Jesus is an important weapon. 'Therefore God also has highly exalted Him and given Him the name which is above every name, that at the name of Jesus every knee should bow, of those in heaven, and of those on earth, and of those under the earth' (Philippians 2:9,10). I recall an account of an Indian, whose mother had told him that if ever he was in danger, there was one name that was more powerful than the name of his gods: that of Jesus. One day, he was sitting on a rock, when a cobra appeared in front of him—ready to strike. He remembered his mother's advice and called 'Jesus', whereupon the cobra turned and slid away. On a particular occasion, we were travelling down a narrow twisting road early in the morning, heading for the airport, to go on a skiing holiday. As we rounded a bend, there was a car on the wrong side of the road—overtaking a lorry and heading straight for us. Don only had time to call 'Jesus', and the car stopped a fraction of an inch in front of us. Then, somehow, it was beside us and driving away. We just caught a glimpse of the man's terrified face as he passed us.

There is power in the name of Jesus. Peter and John demonstrated this when they prayed for the lame man at the gate of the temple called 'Beautiful', and said, '"In the name of Jesus Christ of Nazareth, rise up and walk." And he took him by the right hand and lifted him up, and immediately his feet and ankle bones received strength. So he, leaping up, stood and walked...' (Acts 3:6,7 and see also Acts 3:16a). At Philippi, there was a slave girl with a spirit of divination, who followed Paul and Silas, calling out after them. Paul spoke to the spirit and said, '"I command you in the name of Jesus Christ to come out of her." And he came out that very hour.' (See Acts 16:16–18.)

The blood of Jesus is our most powerful protection against demonic forces. Satan cannot bear us to mention the blood, because that was what defeated him. Many times I have seen demons leave a person as they have been driven out by the mention of the blood of Jesus.

Every time Satan tempted Jesus, he answered him, 'It is written....' If we know the word of God, we can recognise Satan's lies and deception, and we will not be taken in. If, when Satan comes against us, we can say, 'It is written....' then he will leave us—just as he left Jesus.

Prayer and fasting are powerful weapons to use against the enemy. Jesus told the disciples, when they could not cast out a deaf and dumb spirit from a boy, that it would come out only by prayer and fasting. (See Mark 9:29.) There are many stories from the Second World War, concerning the national day of prayer and fasting before the evacuation from Dunkirk. The result was a miraculous calm and the rescue of the soldiers from the beaches, in boats of all kinds. Jehoshaphat also proclaimed a national day of prayer and fasting, when outnumbered by the people of Ammon, Moab and Mount Seir. The result was a miraculous intervention by God, causing the opposing armies to destroy each other. (2 Chronicles 20.)

Praise is another important weapon that we can use against the enemy. Satan hates it when we praise God, because he wanted the praise for himself. He had said, 'I will ascend into heaven, I will exalt my throne above the stars of God.... I will be like the most high' (Isaiah 14:13,14). This is why he was cast out of heaven. When we praise God, not only are we reminded of the greatness of God, but also confusion comes upon the enemy. When King Jehoshaphat's armies were seriously outnumbered, he sent out singers—to go before the army, praising the Lord. 'And when he had consulted with the people, he appointed those who should sing to the LORD, and who should praise the beauty of holiness, as they went out before the army and were saying: "Praise the LORD, For His mercy endures for ever." Now when they began to sing and to praise, the LORD set ambushes against the people of Ammon, Moab, and Mount Seir, who had come against Judah; and they were defeated' (2 Chronicles 20:21,22). Similarly, the walls of Jericho fell down when the people shouted and the priests blew their trumpets. When Paul and Silas sang praises to God, the doors of the prison were opened and their chains fell off. (Acts 16:25,26.) Praise is a powerful weapon. In some way, it releases the power of God to work on our behalf. The Psalmist says, 'But You are holy, enthroned in the praises of Israel' (Psalm 22:3).

Not only do we have weapons for spiritual warfare—we have an armour too. This is described in Ephesians, Chapter Six. We must ensure that our armour is always in place. We must always be wearing the girdle of truth, without which the rest of the armour will fall off! We must not only know the truth, which will set us free, but we must be sure to be wholly truthful in all we do and say. This will keep us safe. The breastplate of righteousness is also described as the breastplate of truth and love. When we understand that in God's sight we are righteous, we will not succumb to the devil's accusations of guilt. Faith is the shield which protects us from the fiery darts of doubt and fear. Finally, the helmet of salvation protects our minds from doubt, fear and confusion, depression, and self-pity: things which would paralyse us from being effective in our fight against the devil. We must be assured of our salvation through Jesus Christ. Then we can say with Paul, 'Now thanks be to God, who always leads us in triumph in Christ, and through us diffuses the fragrance of His knowledge in every place' (2 Corinthians 2:14).

Chapter Nineteen

TEMPTATIONS, TESTS & TRIALS

Yet in all these things we are more than conquerors through Him who loved us.

Romans 8:37

The Greek word *peirasmos*, is variously translated as temptations, tests and trials because it has three distinct meanings: firstly, a trial or proving; secondly, an enticement to sin; and finally, the testing of character or faith. However, in the original text, it is the same word which is used for all three meanings and, therefore, sometimes gives rise to confusion when translated.

James uses all three meanings when he says, 'Blessed is the man who endures temptation' [meaning 'is patient under trial'], 'for when he has been approved,' [i.e. has stood the test and been approved], 'he will receive the crown of life...' (James 1:12–15). He then makes it clear from the context (v.15) that he is talking about enticement to sin in v.13, when he says, 'Let no one say when he is tempted, "I am tempted by God"; for God cannot be tempted by evil nor does He Himself tempt anyone.'

Temptations

God never tempts anyone; it is Satan who is the tempter. (See Matthew 4:3,5.) His aim is to get us to doubt the will of God, the word of God and the goodness of God, so that we are drawn away from the worship of God. Satan desired to be worshipped himself. His temptations centre around three things: the lust of the flesh (appetites, cravings and passions); the lust of the eyes (selfishness and self interest), and the pride of life (self-exaltation). Sadly, the downfall of many Christians in prominent positions has been one of these: sex, money or power. Satan distorted the Scriptures when he tempted Jesus and, as Jesus used the Scriptures to defeat Satan, saying, 'It is written...', he showed that Satan could be defeated.

There are three widely held misconceptions. The first is that temptation is sin. However, this is clearly not the case. Hebrews 4:15 states that Jesus was tempted in all points as we are, 'yet without sin.' James 1:14,15 explains that sin is the result of giving in to temptation. When Satan puts wrong thoughts in our minds, he then tells us we have sinned because we thought like that! What a nerve! He is the accuser of the brethren. We must recognise that the thoughts are not ours but are coming from him. Then we can choose to reject them. However, if we receive them and meditate on them, there is a progression whereby the thought becomes a desire which, as we dwell on it in the imagination, becomes a stronghold. When we allow ourselves to fantasise or meditate on the stronghold, it becomes an obsession, which is uncontrollable. From the moment we receive Satan's thought and make it our own, we are in sin. This is why Jesus said, 'Pray that you may not enter into temptation' (Luke 22:40). Peter tells us to, 'be sober, be vigilant; because your adversary the devil walks about like a roaring lion, seeking whom he may devour' (1 Peter 5:8). It is up to us to, bring, 'every thought into captivity to the obedience of Christ' (2 Corinthians 10:5b).

It is encouraging to note that we are not alone in being tempted, but that temptation is common to all people. However, 1 Corinthians 10:13 suggests that we do not have to be defeated by temptation. We need to be aware that it is possible for us to overcome temptation. 'For sin shall not have dominion over you, for you are not under law but under grace' (Romans 6:14). God has given us weapons and strategies to defeat Satan. Paul tells Timothy that it is best to avoid putting himself in the way of temptation when he tells him to 'flee youthful lusts.' He does not say stand and fight, but flee! Whenever possible, avoid putting yourself in a position where there is opportunity to sin. His advice is to avoid those things which generate strife. We can make it easier for ourselves by being careful about where we go and the company we keep. But not only this: we should also take positive steps both to spend time with those who love the Lord, and to enjoy good things. There is a story told about a fourth century music theorist, who was urged by his neighbours to watch the gladiators perform. Time after time he refused, because of the brutality involved. However, one day he was persuaded and, although he kept his eyes tightly shut, at the sound of a piercing cry, he opened them briefly — only to see one of the fighters receive a fatal wound. This was enough to blunt his finer sensitivities, so that he joined in enthusiastically with the crowd. From then on he was changed from someone who hated violence to someone who enjoyed it. Just one brief encounter was all it took. Often, it is just one step that exposes us to something evil.

It is easier to avoid sin if we are aware of Satan's methods. We need to learn to recognise the temptation for what it is, and to resist it. James tells us that, if we are submitted to God, we shall be able to resist the devil and he will flee. But, if we are double-minded, or in rebellion against God, we shall not be able to resist.

It is important that we do not give Satan any opportunities in our lives through unforgiveness or pride. (See 1 Timothy 3:6.) James describes how envy, self-seeking and lying can lay us open to confusion (James 3:14–16). Paul, in his letter to the Ephesians, associates lying, anger and gossiping with giving place to the devil. (See Ephesians 4:25–27,29.)

The best way to strengthen ourselves against temptation is to be filled with the word of God. (See Psalm119:9,11), and to have the word of God on our lips. Satan will not stay around when we say to him, 'It is written....' After Jesus had quoted Scripture to the devil the third time, '...the devil left Him, and behold, angels came and ministered to Him' (Matthew 4:11). The Bible is the 'sword of the Spirit', with which we are to fight Satan. We are all subject to temptation, but as this, in itself, is not sin, we are not to allow Satan to make us feel guilty about being tempted. The only time we will not be tempted is when we are dead! We do have the ability to resist temptation and, each time we do this, we will become stronger.

Tests

The second misconception is in the area of tests. Tests do not produce faith or increase faith. The only way to get faith is by hearing the word of God. (See Romans 10:17.) Tests merely establish that faith is already present. They reveal the extent of our faith. We cannot have theoretical faith; it must be tested to find out if it is real. The Hebrew word *bachan* means to examine or prove, to see whether a thing is genuine. So Paul says, 'But as we have been approved by God to be entrusted with the gospel, even so we speak, not as pleasing men, but God who tests our hearts' (1 Thessalonians 2:4). God tests to prove that the word is established in us. 'And you shall remember that the LORD your God led you all the way these forty years in the wilderness, to humble you, and test (KJV *prove*) you, to know what was in your heart, whether you would keep His commandments or not' (Deuteronomy 8:2). Satan tests to steal the word from us and make us fail. In Revelation 2:10 we read, '...the devil is about to throw some of you into prison, that you may be tested....' In the garden of Eden, God tested Adam, to see if his love was unconditional. God tested Abraham's faith when He asked him to sacrifice Isaac (God knew, of course, that this would not, in the event, be required or desired.) Abraham proved by his obedience that he would not break his covenant, and God proved to Satan and the world that Abraham would not break his covenant. Satan tested Jesus in the wilderness, to try to make him fail. The Father tested Jesus in the garden of Gethsemane, to prove that he would not fail.

Although tests do not produce faith, when faith is tested it produces patience. (See James 1:3.) If we are asking God for more patience, we had better look out, because the way to get it is by facing tests. It has been well said that, 'if we are in a test, the thing to do is to pass it!' Peter tells us that the way to deal with tests is to rejoice. James says we should be joyful! The word produces joy in our hearts (John 15:11; 1 Thessalonians 1:6). When Satan comes to steal the word, he is trying to steal our joy. If he can do this, he can take our strength, because, 'the joy of the Lord is your strength' (Nehemiah 8:10). If Satan can take our joy, he can defeat us. Consider the response of Habakkuk. Despite disasters, he says, 'Yet I will rejoice in the LORD, I will joy in the God of my salvation' (Habakkuk 3:17–19).

Trials

These may be the same as tests, or they may be trouble, affliction or persecution. The trials mentioned in 1 Peter 4:12 refer to that by which something is tried or proved —a test, and those in 1 Peter 1:7 similarly mean calamities or trials that test the character. These are events we can rejoice in, because they develop patience, helping us to mature.

Then there are afflictions, tribulation, persecution and troubles. These arise for the sake of the gospel, or for the word's sake. 'But recall the former days in which, after you were illuminated, you endured a great struggle with sufferings: partly while you were made a spectacle both by reproaches and tribulations, and partly while you became companions of those who were so treated...' (Hebrews 10:32). As Christians, we must expect a certain amount of persecution. Peter tells us not to be ashamed if we suffer as Christians, but to be sure that we are being reproached for the name of Christ and not because we are causing offence, whether by being 'a busybody' in other people's affairs or because we are doing something else wrong. (See 1 Peter 4:12–16.) It is sad when Christians are disliked because they are gossips or judgemental.

This brings us to the third misconception, which is that all suffering that we go through is God's will. We are to share in the sufferings of Christ *when we are being persecuted as Christians*: sufferings such as rejection, false accusations, or even physical abuse and torture. Paul lists some of the sufferings he has been through for the name of Christ in 2 Corinthians 11:22–28. Psalm 34:19 tells us that, 'Many are the afflictions of the righteous, but the Lord delivers him out of them all.' And Psalm 50:15 exhorts us to, 'Call upon Me [the Lord] in the day of trouble; I will deliver you, and you shall glorify Me.' However, Jesus' suffering at the whipping post and on the cross was on our behalf, so that we do not need to go through the same. In these things, Jesus suffered for us and in our place. These substitutional sufferings are for our sin, sickness and despair. Isaiah 53:4,5 says, 'Surely He has borne our griefs and carried our sorrows... But He was wounded for our transgressions, He was bruised for our iniquities; the chastisement for our peace was upon Him, and by His stripes we are healed.' The literal translation of the words that Isaiah uses for 'griefs and sorrows' means 'sicknesses and pains'. It is not God's will that we should suffer spiritual death for our sins, nor that we should lose our peace, or have disturbed minds, nor that we should be sick. If it were, He would not have sent Jesus to bear these sufferings for us. We must not attribute to God the things that Satan is trying to put upon us. God's desire for us is that we should be whole in body, mind and spirit. Peter describes Jesus as the one, 'Who Himself bore our sins in His own body on the tree, that we, having died to sins, might live for righteousness — by whose stripes you were healed' (1 Peter 2:24). It is sad when people blame God for, or accept as from God, the things that Satan is attacking them with. Again we recall that it is Satan who comes to steal and to kill and to destroy. Jesus came to give us life in abundance.

Chapter Twenty

GROWING UP SPIRITUALLY

...He chose us in Him before the foundation of the world,
that we should be holy and without blame before Him in love.

Ephesians 1:4

When we are born again, at first we are spiritual babies. God's plan
for us is not that we should remain as babies but that, by feeding on
the word, we should grow up to maturity. (Ephesians 4:15). For this
reason, He corrects, disciplines and trains His children. (Hebrews
12:5–11.) A newborn baby is delightful, but a twenty year old be-
having like a baby is not in the least attractive. Therefore, we make
allowances for and help the newborn Christian, but we teach them
the word, so that they can grow up and take responsibility for their
own actions and seek God for themselves. Have you noticed how
easy it is for new Christians to get their prayers answered? As they
grow up, God expects more from them and they have to learn how
to pray in faith, to live in forgiveness, to know God's will, and so
on. Peter exhorts us to, '...grow in the grace and knowledge of our
Lord and Saviour Jesus Christ' (2 Peter 3:18).

A newborn baby is dependent, demanding and self-centred.
Hebrews 5:13 says that the baby Christian is 'unskilled in the word
of righteousness', because he feeds only on milk. A baby is
undiscerning, tending to put everything in his mouth. We need to
ensure that new Christians are receiving wholesome, digestible food.
For the new Christians, 'milk' must be supplied so that they grow.
(See 1 Peter 2:2). This pure spiritual milk consists of the elemen-
tary principles described in Hebrews 6:1, namely, the foundations
of the faith — 'repentance from dead works', [works cannot save
us], 'faith toward God' [we are saved by faith through Christ Jesus],
'baptisms' [as a declaration of our new birth, and the baptism in the

89

Holy Spirit], 'laying on of hands', 'resurrection of the dead', and teaching about 'eternal judgement'. It is important for new Christians to be established, understanding basic teaching, before feeding on 'meat'. Peter explains the danger in 2 Peter 3:16,17, when he writes: 'Paul....speaking in them [his epistles] of these things, in which are some things hard to understand, which untaught and unstable people twist to their own destruction, as they do also the rest of the Scriptures.' It is important not to build doctrine on one verse of Scripture—it must be substantiated by several, and cohere with the principles found throughout the whole of the Bible. Moreover, it is important not to overemphasise certain aspects of doctrine, falsely opposing them to others. Once the basic doctrines have been learnt, it is important that the 'baby' should progress to solid food.

Childhood is characterised by our being easily influenced, inquisitive but lacking discernment, easily hurt, and talkative. Having established the basic principles, we must leave these and 'go on to perfection' (Hebrews 6:1). Ephesians 4:14 describes children as being, 'carried about with every wind of doctrine, by the trickery of men....' Young Christians must be taught to evaluate everything by the word of God. Ephesians was written by Paul in order to bring the church to maturity. He taught that they would grow up by learning to speak the truth in love. The maturing Christian is shown much about the dangers of the uncontrolled tongue. James warns against careless, destructive use of the tongue— gossiping, speaking evil of another; and against boasting. He says that only a mature person has learned to control the tongue.

Ephesians 4:13–23 gives a description of the mature person. Such a person is no longer self-conscious, but God-conscious. He has an accurate knowledge of the Son of God, and has come to know God as his Father. He is able to discern good and evil, having been fed on solid food, and having habitually exercised his senses in line with the word. As 1 Thessalonians 5:21 says, 'Test all things; hold fast what is good.' Becoming mature, in this sense, has little to do with how long ago you were converted! It has far more to do with the closeness of your walk with Jesus, openness to the Holy Spirit, knowledge of God's word, and obedience to it. The mature Christian knows how to use the word of God correctly, not twisting it to back up futile arguments, in the way described in 2 Timothy 2:16,23 and 4:3 but, rather, with a thorough understanding of Biblical principles and teaching. He does not seek after signs, but believes the word of God to be enough for all situations. He does not seek after experiences, good though they might be, but seeks to know more of God Himself. As Paul said, 'That I may know Him and the power of His resurrection, and the fellowship of His sufferings, being conformed to His death' (Philippians 3:10). Paul came to the point at which he could say, 'I also count all things loss for the excellence of the knowledge of Christ Jesus my Lord...' (Philippians 3:8).

A mature Christian holds earthly things lightly, like Moses being ready to give up the riches of Egypt's royal family, becoming a refugee with the children of Israel, because that was what God had called him to do. Complete obedience to God is what characterises the mature Christian.

A spiritual man is not easily offended; he does not respond badly to criticism, and is concerned only about what God thinks of him. Nor does he seek the praise of men, but does all for the glory of God. As a young boy, Joseph was proud, arrogant and insensitive, bragging to his brothers about his dreams, and parading in the special coat that his father gave him. He was far from ready for the fulfilment of the dreams. Nonetheless, throughout his time in slavery and in prison, God was with him, preparing him for leadership of the nation. Unjustly imprisoned, he did not say, 'it's unfair'; forgotten by those he had helped, he did not get into self pity or resentment. When he eventually came before Pharaoh, he was ready for the job for which God had prepared him—to become ruler over Pharaoh's household, and over the land of Egypt. Now, he showed that he was able to handle not only disappointment but also success, as he gave all the glory to God. He had learnt humility, so that when Pharaoh called him and asked him to interpret his dream, Joseph said, 'It is not in me; God will give Pharaoh an answer of peace.' (Genesis 41:16). Finally, when faced with the brothers who had sold him into slavery, he not only forgave them, but even tried to make it easier for them saying, 'Do not therefore be grieved or angry with yourselves because you sold me here; for God sent me before you

GROWING IN THE WORD

to preserve life' (Genesis 45:5).

Whereas a baby Christian (of any age!) may still think as the world thinks, a mature Christian has learnt to 'have the mind of Christ.' He no longer measures things by the world's standards, but sees things from a spiritual point of view; he no longer responds to setbacks with panic or despair, but has confidence in God to see him through. When trials come, the spiritual man sees them as an opportunity to overcome, and rejoices. He knows that this produces patience, which leads to greater maturity. He has learnt to look to God rather than looking at the circumstances, and to be more influenced by what the word says than by feelings. He knows how to give the 'sacrifice of praise', because our Father God is always worthy of our praise, and praising God does not depend on how we are feeling.

There is only one way to become mature. It is to know the word and to be obedient to it. Paul writes to Timothy, 'All Scripture is given by inspiration of God, and is profitable for doctrine, for reproof, for correction, for instruction in righteousness, that the man of God may be complete, thoroughly equipped for every good work' (2 Timothy 3:16,17). Romans 12:9–21 gives an excellent description of what the life of mature Christians should be like. The test of maturity is the fruit. 'Therefore by their fruits you will know them' (Matthew 7:20). Only a mature and healthy tree produces fruit. It grows strong and healthy by being planted in good soil. Jesus said, 'Abide in Me, and I in you. As the branch cannot bear fruit of itself, unless it abides in the vine, neither can you, unless you abide in Me.... He who abides in Me, and I in him, bears much fruit; for without Me you can do nothing' (John 15:4,5). Just as a mature tree naturally produces fruit, so a mature Christian does not struggle to produce fruit, but does so naturally—if he abides in the Lord. It is the word in us that produces the fruit, '...the word of the truth of the gospel, which has come to you, as it has also in all the world, and is bringing forth fruit...' (Colossians 1:5,6). Paul prays for the Christians in Colosse, '...that you may be filled with the knowledge of His will in all wisdom and spiritual understanding; that you may walk worthy of the Lord, fully pleasing Him, being fruitful in every good work and increasing in the knowledge of God; strengthened

GROWING UP SPIRITUALLY

with all might, according to His glorious power, for all patience and longsuffering with joy; giving thanks to the Father who has qualified us to be partakers of the inheritance of the saints in the light' (Colossians 1:9-13). Walking in love is the most important fruit of the mature Christian life. (See 1 Corinthians 13:4-8.)

APPENDIX

The Tabernacle

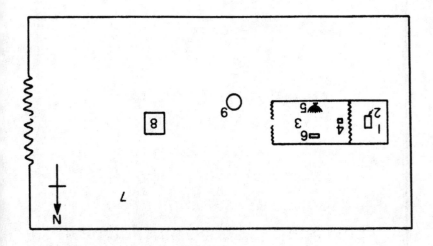

1. *The Most Holy Place, sometimes called the 'Holy of Holies'*
2. *The Ark of the Covenant*
3. *The Holy Place*
4. *Altar of Incense*
5. *The Lampstand*
6. *The Table*
7. *The Courtyard*
8. *The Altar of Burnt Offering*
9. *The Basin*

From The Way of the Spirit, Volume One, The Call and the Cross, 1993, pg 120.
Used by kind permission of John McKay and Kingdom Faith Ministries.

An ideal resource for group
teaching and personal Bible study,
on the themes covered by
Growing in the Word:

TOWARDS CHRISTIAN MATURITY
THE COURSE MANUAL
by
Hilary Latham

Convenient, spiral bound
A4 format
Ample space for notes
80 pages

ISBN 0953149412

Obtainable by post from:
Don Latham Associates
P.O. Box 1834
Bradford on Avon, Wiltshire BA15 2YA
Telephone (01225) 867778

A FAITH THAT WORKS
by Don Latham

The author has seen many people born again, filled with
the Holy Spirit—and often healed— as he ministers.
Writing with wide professional experience, as Chief Executive
of a local authority, now a non-executive Director of Wiltshire
Health Authority, Don Latham teaches about exercising faith
in the whole of life—including the workplace.
ISBN 1901949001   £6.99

BOOKS BY PETER H. LAWRENCE:

DOING WHAT COMES SUPERNATURALLY
Learning how to minister in the power of the Holy Spirit
Extremely useful for ministers and church members who
want to learn more about ministering—includes teaching
on healing and deliverance. Packed with good, biblical sense.
ISBN 0952268841   £5.99

THE HOT LINE
How can we hear God speak—today?
Preface by Michael Green Foreword by David Pytches
A local parish church moves into renewal. People begin to
hear words from God. Issues such as healing and ministering
to the demonised begin to arise. How do we discern what is
from God? This classic account is described by the author as
'a beginner's book, written by a beginner for beginners.'
ISBN 0952268868   £5.99

CHRISTIAN HEALING
A thoroughly biblical and practical approach. How Jesus healed
the sick; how the disciples healed the sick; how we can minister
for healing, in the power of the Holy Spirit. Excellent value—
ideal for teaching, and for ministry teams
ISBN 0952268876   £3.95

AVAILABLE FROM CHRISTIAN BOOKSHOPS
Terra Nova Publications   www.kings-books.com/terranova.htm